AN OUTLINE OF THE RUMANIAN CAMPAIGN, 1916-18

by

Major-General W. M. St. G. Kirke, C.B., C.M.G., D.S.O., *p.s.c.*

The Naval & Military Press Ltd

Reproduced by kind permission of the Central Library,
Royal Military Academy, Sandhurst

Published by
The Naval & Military Press Ltd
Unit 10, Ridgewood Industrial Park,
Uckfield, East Sussex,
TN22 5QE England
Tel: +44 (0) 1825 749494
Fax: +44 (0) 1825 765701
www.naval-military-press.com
www.military-genealogy.com

© The Naval & Military Press Ltd 2010

The Naval & Military Press ...

...offer specialist books for the serious student of conflict. The range of titles stocked covers the whole spectrum of military history with titles on uniforms, battles, official histories, specialist works containing Medal Rolls and Casualties Lists, and numismatic titles for medal collectors and researchers.

The innovative approach they have to military bookselling and their commitment to publishing have made them Britain's leading independent military bookseller.

In reprinting in facsimile from the original, any imperfections are inevitably reproduced and the quality may fall short of modern type and cartographic standards.

THE JOURNAL
OF THE
Royal United Service Institution.

VOL. LXIX.   NOVEMBER, 1924.   No. 476.

[Authors alone are responsible for the contents of their respective Papers. All communications (except those for perusal by the Editor only) should be addressed to the Secretary, Royal United Service Institution.]

AN OUTLINE OF THE RUMANIAN CAMPAIGN, 1916–1918.

By MAJOR-GENERAL W. M. ST. G. KIRKE, C.B., C.M.G., D.S.O., *p.s.c.*

I.

THE Rumanian campaign and, more particularly, the opening phases, is of special interest to the British Army, in that it was essentially a war of movement, fought in varying conditions of *terrain* and climate, between forces of moderate size.

The handling of infantry divisions, or even brigades, of small bodies of cavalry or artillery in circumstances which gave full scope to the initiative of subordinate commanders, frequently had a determining effect in important actions. In the later stages, as the forces on both sides increased, and the frontage to be defended contracted, the campaign assumed the well-known characteristics of the Western front.

Within the compass of a few articles it is obviously impossible to deal fully with a campaign lasting intermittently for two years. It is, therefore, the intention to concentrate rather on the strategy and on the more interesting actions of the earlier phases, and to summarise the remainder sufficiently only to enable the reader to fit Rumania's part into the general picture of the world war.

One of the minor difficulties which is encountered in dealing with this campaign is that of nomenclature. Most places in Transylvania have German, Rumanian, and Magyar names, those on the Bulgarian side have Rumanian and Bulgarian designations, whilst some have been anglicised in English accounts. It is hoped, however, that reference to the accompanying maps will avoid any ambiguity on this score.

Much has been written, and remains to be written, as to why Rumania did not openly range herself on the side of the allies at an earlier stage; what would have been the effect had she done so, and so forth. With this we are not here concerned.

The political and military circumstances in which she declared war on 27th August, 1916, must, however, be understood, as they had an important bearing on her initial strategy, which is the first problem for our consideration.

POLITICAL FACTORS.

The following lines do not pretend to be in any way a complete account of the protracted negotiations leading to the declaration of war.

Rumania had clear-cut national aspirations; towards their fulfilment she had made a promising start when, in 1913, she had acquired an additional slice of the Dobrudja from Bulgaria without firing a shot, by the simple process of waiting until the other Balkan States had fought first Turkey, and then each other, to a standstill.

There remained the Rumanian *irridenta* of Transylvania (Austrian), the Banat (Austrian), Bukovina (Austrian), and Bessarabia (Russian). (*See* map number 2.)

A satisfactory offer as regards the two former as the price of intervention had always been open, but the Bukovina was a more difficult matter. However, in 1916, the natural aversion of a strong Power like Russia to ceding territory which she herself desired had at last been overcome. (Bessarabia was eventually acquired as an unexpected bonus.)

Public sentiment which, in 1914, had been by no means unanimously on the side of the Entente Powers, owing to distrust of Russia, was in 1916 flowing strongly in their favour.

The crushing of Serbia, Rumania's friend of 1913, a waning belief in the invincibility of Germany were contributory causes, but perhaps the most powerful influence was the dire situation of their compatriots in Transylvania, where the ruthless methods of the Austrian Chief of Police far surpassed anything experienced by the Belgians at the hands of the Germans.

Politically, therefore, Rumania was ripe for intervention; the only question was—when? This would naturally depend on the general military situation.

MILITARY CONSIDERATIONS.

Given a free choice, Rumania naturally wished to launch her army on the crest of the wave; more than this, she appreciated the fact that militarily she was but a pigmy, that she was in danger of isolation, and that it was risky in the extreme to intervene in a struggle of giants unless one of them was holding her hand. In June and July, 1916, events appeared to be shaping themselves favourably. On every side the Central Powers had been thrown on to the defensive. In the West the abortive German offensive at Verdun had been succeeded by successful French counterattacks, and by the battle of the Somme. Reports from that side were not deficient in optimism as to the effect of these battles on German military man power and resources.

The Austrian offensive in the Tyrol initiated on May 15th had petered out, and the Italians were attacking with success on the Isonzo.

On the Salonica front the Bulgarian offensive, designed to deter Rumania from joining the allies, had been broken off owing to events in Galicia, and Sarrail was himself preparing to attack.

Lastly Brussilof, in June, had, as Hindenburg puts it, commenced " tapping the enemy " all along their eastern front from the Pripet to Rumania, until he had broken through on a wide front in Galicia, and had swept the Austrians out of the Bukovina and up to the Carpathians, beyond which lay the fertile plains of Hungary. The Austrian retreat was only stayed by throwing in German troops which had been earmarked for a counteroffensive on another portion of the Russian front. The fact that no preparation had been made by the Russians to exploit this spectacular but somewhat unexpected success was not immediately apparent, though possibly it may have accounted for their decision to join the other allies in pressing Rumania to enter the war at this juncture. Hitherto General Alexieff had not considered that any extension of the Russian front by the entry of Rumania into the war would be to the allies' advantage, preferring the flank protection afforded by her neutrality to the assistance of her army.

The intimation that this was the psychological moment was conveyed in no uncertain terms. The Rumanians were told that it was " Now or Never," and on their decision depended their hopes of territorial aggrandisement.

Rumania complied, after some haggling over certain political and financial conditions, by which valuable time was lost, and amid scenes of great national enthusiasm declared war on Austria-Hungary on 27th August. Germany followed suit on the following day; the attitude of Bulgaria remained uncertain.

In the military convention giving effect to agreements arrived at with the allies, the more important points were the following :—

  (a) Energetic action by the Russians, particularly in the Bukovina, against the Austrians;
  (b) Co-operation by the Russian Fleet in the Black Sea;
  (c) Two Russian infantry divisions and one cavalry division to be sent on the first day of mobilisation to the Dobrudja, to be increased as and when necessary;
  (d) A minimum of 300 tons of munitions to reach Rumania daily;

(e) An allied offensive on the Salonika front to be initiated practically simultaneously with the Rumanian entry into the war.

THE RUMANIAN ARMY.

The numbers available on the outbreak of hostilities are shown in Appendix A. Since the outbreak of the great war, Rumania had made strenuous efforts to increase the strength and efficiency of her army, in the face of great difficulties. Chief of these was her isolation, which prevented the provision of up-to-date equipment, or even of the first essentials for her greatly expanded army. Requirements of countries which had already entered the war on the side of the allies naturally received priority over one which had not yet taken the decisive step. Moreover, Rumania's only access to her allies, other than Russia—which could supply nothing—was viâ Archangel and Murmansk and thence across Russia, who herself was in chronic need of warlike stores.

It was not, therefore, surprising that the vast majority of munitions intended for Rumania, both before and after the declaration of war, failed to arrive at their destination.

The Rumanian Army, consisting of 23 divisions, 2 cavalry divisions, and 5 *calarasi* (Yeomanry) brigades, though a formidable weapon on paper, was not equipped even up to our 1914 standard. If the old regular divisions 1 to 10 were good, the newer formations (11 to 15) were indifferent, whilst 16 to 23 formed on mobilisation were worse.

Her total available rifles amounted to 300,000 Männlicher and 250,000 converted Martini-Henrys. Whilst divisions numbers 1 to 10 had two machine-guns per battalion, or six per regiment, divisions numbers 11 to 15 had only two per regiment, and divisions 16 to 23 none at all.

There was nothing corresponding to the Lewis gun, the *fusil mitrailleuse*, or the German light machine gun.

Thus, although infantry battalions were 1,000 to 1,200 strong, their fire power was actually considerably inferior to that of the far weaker German units.

The large number of battalions in an infantry division (15 to 25) made the division (20,000 to 25,000) an unwieldy formation, and greatly increased the problems of movement and supply over the exiguous communications in the mountain regions, without a commensurate gain in fire power.

In artillery she had 180 (4-gun) batteries of field artillery, grouped into regiments of six batteries, one regiment of horse artillery, and one of mountain artillery. To increase her small amount of heavy artillery she had drawn on the fixed defences of Bucharest and Galatz and on the fleet. In all, she could put 1,400 guns of very varying models and efficiency into the field.

No gas equipment, offensive or defensive, was available, no trench mortars and very few telephones.

Her air forces were negligible and she had no anti-aircraft guns or lights.

For all natures of ammunition she was mainly dependant on outside sources and consequently the six weeks' supply with which she started the campaign quickly vanished when the promised 300 tons daily did not materialise with any regularity. In addition, an explosion in Bucharest arsenal on 28th May—engineered, it is said, by a Bulgar—destroyed nine million rounds of small arms ammunition and ten out of thirteen cartridge-filling machines.

A survey of the facts leads one to doubt whether the Rumanian Army had gained any military advantage by delay in entering the war.

Efficiency is a relative term, and though Rumania had more than doubled her forces, all her efforts during her two years of preparation had not improved the training and equipment of her army relative to that of her adversaries, owing to the lack of mechanical aids and ignorance of the new methods which had been developed in the meanwhile.

In this respect the Germans had almost as great an advantage as against the Austrians in 1866, or the Russians in 1914 and 1915.

The great expansion of the Rumanian Army led to yet one further difficulty. The proportion of the *intelligentsia* in Rumania is not large, and it was impossible to provide an adequate number of good subordinate leaders. The corps of officers, increased from the 600 of 1913 to 20,000, contained a proportion of inefficients which, in the event, proved that the expansion had been overdone. Thus the Rumanian Army lacked the first essential for a large expansion, viz., strong and well trained cadres.

The bravery of the individual Rumanian soldier could not compensate for such disabilities, and the appalling losses suffered in the first four months of the campaign may largely be traced to the above causes.

The lesson is obvious. If mechanism depends on the spirit and efficiency of the man who works it, the man's efficiency is no less dependent on that of the machine. The two are interdependent. God, as in the days of Napoleon, is still doubtless on the side of the big battalions, but size must now be read in terms of fire-power and movement, as well as in bayonets. The Rumanian attempt to oppose bullets by human bodies could only have one result.

The Theatre of Operations.

Map number 1 shows the general theatre of operations better than pages of description. It will be seen that the fertile plains of Rumania lie like an oasis in the tangle of mountains which characterise the *terrain* of Transylvania, the Bukovina, and, to a lesser extent, the Dobrudja and Bulgaria. On the south, the Danube—unbridged except at Cernavoda—separated Rumania from Bulgaria or territory in Bulgarian occupation from Orsova on the west until ten miles west of Turtukai, whence the frontier ran across the Dobrudja to the Black

Sea. On this latter section there was no natural protection. The points to note about this frontier are that:—

(1) The unbridged Danube is a formidable obstacle, though the various islands afford facilities for assembling bridging material.

(2) The Bulgarian bank commands the Rumanian bank throughout.

(3) The fortresses of Turtukai and Silistria, designed originally by Bulgaria to protect her frontier, formed excellent jumping-off points for a Rumanian offensive, but defensively were a weakness, as Turtukai was unconnected by bridge, and Silistria only by a pontoon bridge, with the Rumanian railheads on the north bank.

(4) The above remark applies very largely to the whole Rumanian Dobrudja. Defensively the best line was just south of, and covering, the Cernavoda–Constanza railway, or a flank position for a striking force based on Turtukai and Silistria.

The length of this southern frontier was about two hundred and seventy miles of river and ninety miles of land front.

The northern frontier ran in a great arc of some four hundred miles from the Russian left flank at Dorna Vatra to Orsova along the crests of the Transylvanian Alps. This mountain barrier, rising to over eight thousand feet, sinks gradually towards the plains of the Danube, throwing out long spurs into Rumania, whilst on the Transylvanian side it falls much more abruptly down into the valleys of the Maros and Olt.

Beyond this moat-like depression, with its circular road and railway, lay a succession of further mountain barriers, the first of which facing east (the Gurghilui range)[1] was backed by a good network of roads and railways; railheads at Reghinul Sasesc (Szasz Regen), Praid (Paradj), Szekely-Udvarhely, Brasov (Kronstadt).

These lines ran back to junctions along the lateral line Des, Cluj (Klausenburg), Alba Julia (Karlsburg), and Hatszeg (Hötzing), which again connected with the main Hungarian railway system.

Looking at the country from the point of view of a Rumanian offensive, it will be seen that the main mountain barrier is pierced by a number of passes, beginning on the west with the Iron Gates through which passes the Danube, the best enemy line of supply. Through all these passes, except the Vulcan Pass, ran good roads. In addition the Red Tower (Turnul Rosu or Rother Turm) Pass, the cleft formed by the Olt River, carried the railway to Sibiu (Hermannstadt). Further east lies a centre group of six passes (E-K) all converging on Brasov (Kronstadt), of which the Predeal (Tomos) Pass carried the main line from Bucharest.

Northwards, round the corner, are further passes, of which the most important is the Ghimes Pass, over which ran the Trotus valley railway.

All these passes played a more or less important part in the campaign. In addition there were a number of tracks which, curiously enough, were

---

[1] Gorgeny Gebirge on Panorama Map I.

made more use of by the Austro-Germans than by the Rumanians, whose peace training had neglected mountain warfare.

Turning to communications in Rumania itself (Map 3), we see at once that the railway system left much to be desired. This was due mainly to the shape of the country and, to a less extent, to the long spurs previously mentioned, which tended to discourage the construction of lateral railways close to the frontier.

Thus on the Transylvania front, transference of troops from one point to another had to be carried out round an arc involving hundreds of miles—very much the situation on the allied Western front—but in Wallachia there was only one line of railway and that single. Northern Moldavia was rather better off, having two alternative routes.

In Wallachia the situation was aggravated owing to the fact that a projected line, Bucharest-Rosi de Vede-Craiova, had not been constructed and consequently the only railway communication zig-zagged *viâ* Pitesti. As a concrete instance of the general effect, the distance from the Predeal Pass to the Red Tower (Rother Turm) Pass by the Rumanian railways was two hundred and seventy miles as compared with eighty miles by the Transylvanian system.

The excessive length and shape of her exposed frontiers, combined with the weakness of her communications, thus robbed Rumania of the advantages which the possession of interior lines *vis-à-vis* Austria and Bulgaria might otherwise have conferred on her. This was particularly the case if she were thrown on to the defensive. Passive defence with twenty-three divisions along a frontier of over seven hundred miles was obviously out of the question, and the situation demanded offensive action if only as a defensive measure.

Only one further factor now remains to be considered, viz., the enemy, before coming to the first great problems. Where and how should the Rumanian offensive have been launched?

THE ENEMY.

The situation which presented itself to the Rumanian general staff was as follows (*see* map number 2):

On the Transylvanian frontier were only weak detachments of Austrian troops (five divisions), sent to a quiet front to recuperate and reform.

In the Bukovina and Galicia the Russian advance was temporarily suspended on the slopes of the Carpathians, but a renewed offensive was promised in conjunction with any Rumanian attack into Transylvania. Austria was held to be incapable of further effort and here the unknown factor was the extent to which Germany could send reinforcements, and when. Ultimately it was possible that Rumania might have to deal with a considerable number of German divisions, judging by the capacity of the railways, but the allies hoped to be able to hold the majority on other fronts by continuing their offensives. On the southern front were two strong Bulgarian divisions, and four cavalry brigades, backed by a portion of one German division (101st)—say, 70,000–75,000 troops—with 30,000–40,000 more watching the crossings of the Danube.

If, contrary to expectations, the Bulgarians intervened, then the pressure exerted by General Sarrail on the Salonica front would determine how far the enemy could increase their forces south of the Danube. On this point the Rumanian general staff had received from Marshal Joffre the most definite assurances.[1]

The initiative, therefore, lay with the Rumanian Army of over half a million men for a period which depended partly on the action of the other allies but more perhaps on the success of her own opening moves. How she should have used it is a question which has been hotly debated.

The Rumanian Plan.

Two main alternatives were open, the first a main offensive in the south, which entailed a defensive attitude on the Transylvanian frontier; the second an advance into Transylvania with a corresponding defensive *vis-à-vis* Bulgaria. The advantages of the former were very great from the point of view of the allies, and indirectly for Rumania also. If Bulgaria, whose policy was thought to be shaky, could be eliminated, Germany's communications with Turkey would be cut, and our heavy liabilities in eastern theatres would soon be liquidated.

Moreover the difficult problem of supply both to Russia and Rumania would be solved by the opening of easy routes from the Mediterranean, and a term would be put to the extremely unsatisfactory situation on the Salonika front.

A successful advance into Bulgaria might have finished the war and, though this was not foreseen at the time, have avoided the Russian revolution, with all its unfortunate consequences.

It promised, in fact, all those advantages which the abortive campaign in Gallipoli had failed to secure, and it is not surprising that the British general staff should have favoured it.

From the Rumanian standpoint, however, there were disadvantages. An advance into Bulgaria was a serious undertaking, particularly if the Bulgarians fought delaying actions back to the rugged barriers of the Balkan mountains which effectively covered Sofia, until Germany could intervene. Sarrail was a very long way off, and had shown little signs of being able to push back the enemy over the mountainous regions, where nature was against him. Unless the Rumanian Army could join hands with him, it would still be isolated and Rumania itself exposed to attack from the N.W. Bucharest was only 70 miles from the frontier, and an Austro-German advance through the Brasov group of passes would have cut Rumania in half and severed the communications of her armies operating south of the Danube unless Russia intervened in force. But if Russia could spare large forces, why should they not invade Bulgaria? It was presumably by some such course of reasoning that Rumania arrived

---

[1] The possibility of Turkish troops co-operating does not appear to have been contemplated.

at the conclusion that she would only co-operate in an attack on Bulgaria if 250,000 Russians were employed for the purpose. Such a force Russia had no intention of supplying, probably because she knew that Brussilov's success was more spectacular than real, and that there was nothing much behind it.

She therefore favoured the second alternative, which would directly relieve pressure on her own front.

The military advantages of an offensive into Transylvania were, firstly, that by advancing to the chord of the arc formed by the Rumanian frontier the latter would be shortened by over 100 miles. Secondly, if the lateral railway line Des–Hatszeg were seized or denied to the enemy the situation as regards communications would be more or less equalised; and, lastly, the barrier of the Carpathians, which had always stopped the Russians, would be turned and Brussilov could continue his victorious career into the plains of Hungary, holding Rumania's hand.

Politically the Balkan Powers have always been great believers in the " bird in the hand " doctrine. It dictated the Bulgarian strategy also, and gave the Germans much trouble.

Psychologically an advance into Transylvania would raise the *morale* of the Rumanian people, and therefore of the army, as nothing else could do. For them it was what Alsace-Lorraine was to the French, or Trieste to the Italians.

Everything, therefore, pointed to this course and if it was wrong the Russians must share the blame, as they pressed for it.

In any case it was finally sanctioned by Marshal Joffre, who at that time was endeavouring to co-ordinate allied action on all fronts.

The fact that the plan broke down at an early stage does not prove that the alternative would have been any more successful if characterised by the many faults of execution which will appear later.

There remained the question of holding the southern front. The Rumanian Government had indeed originally stipulated for 150,000 Russian troops, in which case she was ready to declare war on Bulgaria. However, General Alexieff, C.G.S. of the Russian Army, considered that he could make better use of them elsewhere, and eventually a compromise was reached by which two infantry divisions and one cavalry division were to move into the Dobrudja on the declaration of war. The Russian Military Authorities admitted later that they had underestimated the extent of the Bulgarian danger and should have sent more. It has been represented that it was Russia which lulled Rumania into a false sense of security as regards Bulgaria's attitude, but it appears from the evidence that Russia joined the other allies in pressing Rumania to include Bulgaria in the declaration of war, and that the negotiations nearly broke down owing to Rumania's reluctance to do so.

Apparently the latter's politicians hoped to compensate for military weakness on the southern frontier by the chance that Bulgaria might not attack her, forgetting that if such a course was in Rumania's interests it must be contrary to those of the Central Powers.

Subsequent events showed that, strategically, the resulting un
certainty as regards Bulgaria's attitude was a cardinal error.

The Rumanian Strategic Deployment.
(*See* map number 3.)

We will now examine the measures taken to carry out the Rumanian plan, starting with the offensive (Transylvanian) front. The latter was 400 miles long and the first point would apparently be to decide over what front the advance should be conducted and whether the main strength should be on the right or left flank.

The advantages of advancing with the left in strength appear to be that this was the most direct route into the Maros valley, and would cut a considerable proportion of the railways feeding the defensive front further east, which the enemy must then evacuate. It would be dangerous to advance with weak forces, because it was the portion of the front against which the enemy could most easily concentrate.

On the other hand, though there was a through line to Sibiu (Hermannstadt), the communications in western Wallachia were poor, and the roads through the mountains limited to those in the Olt, Jiu, and Cerna valleys, forty to fifty miles apart. Further, Rumania's intervention was based on the assumption that the Russians would advance from the north, consequently a Rumanian advance from western Wallachia would be in the nature of an isolated movement. (*See* map No. 1.)

For an advance from northern Moldavia, the railway system behind the front was considerably better, and there was a through railway over the Ghimes pass.[1] On the other hand it entailed a much longer advance over equally difficult country, including a frontal attack on the inner bastion of mountains, before the main Maros valley was reached at Reghinul-Sasesc (Szasz-Regen) and Maros Vasahely.

As previously mentioned, this bastion was backed by a good road and railway system and was likely to be held by the enemy. However, the Russian advance should help to overcome this difficulty.

In principle the Rumanian general staff adopted the advance by the right wing and centre, pivoting on a base to be formed by the First Army in the west. But it does not appear that any concerted plan was made with the Russians—if it was, the Russians did not carry out their part—and consequently the Rumanian operation became an independent one.

To come to actual details, the offensive armies were organised as follows:—

> *First Army* (General Culcer), divisions numbers 1, 11, 13, with 2nd, 12th and 23rd (forming) in reserve, and a Calarasi brigade. Total effectives, 134,403.

---

[1] This was irreparably broken by the retiring Austrians.

Second Army (General Averescu), divisions numbers 3, 4, 5, 6, and 1st cavalry, a Calarasi brigade and the 21st and 22nd divisions forming in reserve. Total effectives, 126,808.

Fourth (Northern Army) (General Presan), divisions numbers 8, 7, 14, and 2nd cavalry; 4th and 38th Brigades and a Calarasi brigade. Total effectives, 107,948.

In general reserve for either front, near Bucharest, divisions numbers 10 and 15, and the Heavy Artillery. Total effectives, 51,165.

The objective of the above was nominally the line shown on map number 2, though probably the High Command hardly expected to get so far.

It is difficult to trace in this arrangement any sign of a strong marching right wing. Rather would it appear that the allocation of forces was dictated entirely by the capacity of the communications, which were best in the centre; possibly also by a latent desire to cover Bucharest, which dominated Rumanian strategy throughout. In any case it involved a gigantic wheel by isolated columns on a front of some three hundred miles, and was more in the nature of a forward concentration than an offensive operation. It could only be justified on one of two assumptions: either that no serious opposition would be met with until concentration was complete, or that each column had behind it sufficient reserves to ensure it against defeat in detail.

The first assumption would probably have been correct had Rumania declared war a few weeks earlier, whilst Germany was still fully employed in stabilising the Austro-Russian front; the second might have been justified but for events in the south which led to the removal of all the reserves from behind the Transylvanian offensive.

THE SOUTHERN FRONT.

For defence against any possible action by Bulgaria the following were allotted:—the 17th division, Turtukai; the 9th division, Silistria and the Dobrudja front; the 19th division, Constanza and the Dobrudja front; the 16th, 18th, 20th divisions, along the Danube.

These troops constituted the Third Army, their total effectives being 142,523.

In addition, two Russian[1] infantry and one cavalry divisions were on the move to the Dobrudja front.

With the general reserve so near as Bucharest, these forces should have been ample.

It has been stated[2] that it was the intention, if attacked, to fight delaying actions back to positions covering the Constanza–Cernavoda railway, until the Russians arrived, and eventually to advance and seize the line Ruscuk–Sumla–Varna (*see* map number 2) as an additional protection to Bucharest.

---

[1] One of these Divisions was formed from Serbian prisoners of war.
[2] "Istoria Rozbouilui," by Const. Kiritescu, vol. 1, p. 166.

Except that in both cases it was apparently assumed that Turtukai and Silistria could take care of themselves, it is hard to find in the preliminary dispositions signs of any such plan; rather they disclose a dispersion of force which, in an attempt to hold everything, left them weak everywhere, in the face of a far smaller but concentrated enemy.

Air observation of any kind would probably have given them sufficient confidence in their intelligence to avoid this elementary mistake.

THE GERMAN COUNTERMEASURES. (*See* map number 2.)

The Germans had not been blind to the possibility of Rumanian intervention. At the end of July parts of the 101st German division were transferred to Ruscuk on the Rumanian frontier and Mackensen was informed, that in the event of war with Rumania, he was to take over command on the Dobrudja and Danube fronts. Meantime he was to make such reconnaissances and preparations as were possible without attracting attention.

It was assumed that Rumania would advance into Transylvania and, as the result of conferences between German, Austrian, Bulgarian, and Turkish representatives, countermeasures were based on that hypothesis. Mackensen, with a new army consisting of part of 101st German division, four Bulgarian divisions (including one to come from Macedonia) and two Turkish divisions from Adrianople, was to attack as soon as possible in the Dobrudja with a view to a subsequent crossing of the Danube and an advance on Bucharest. With this in view the Austrian heavy Danube bridging train was sent to near Sistovo, where it was hidden behind an island. The technical difficulties of crossing further down stream were considered to be too great. Preparations were also made " for the abundant equipment of Mackensen's Army with such weapons, not yet known to the Rumanians, as heavy artillery, mine-throwers, gas." (Falkenhayn.)[1]

In the north, Falkenhayn, who was then C.G.S., says that the Austrians were to try to hold up the advance of the main Rumanian forces over the mountains as long as possible, until the attacking troops which were to be despatched immediately after the declaration of war had got into position. Germany had earmarked five infantry divisions and between one and two cavalry divisions to help in this. Austrian headquarters intended to send to Transylvania two infantry divisions and one cavalry division, all of which had suffered heavily in battles on the eastern front, but which could be brought up to strength. Unity of command on the Rumanian front from the Danube to the Bukovina was assured by placing the Austrian first army already in Transylvania under General Arz von Strausenburg, whose orders were to organise southern Hungary for defence, block the passes, and prepare demolitions. Falkenhayn complains that the Italian offensive at the beginning of August interfered with the proper execution of these latter orders.

---

[1] "Der Feldzug der 9. Armee gegen die Rumänen und Russen, 1916–1919."

Hindenburg, who replaced Falkenhayn on the outbreak of the war with Rumania, accepted these arrangements without serious modification.

The only element of surprise was that a Rumanian declaration of war was not expected until after the harvest in the middle of September, but Falkenhayn says that it only required a few telegrams to complete the counterpreparations, which were all well advanced. Hindenburg, on the contrary, says that, owing to the situation on other fronts, " the Rumanian declaration of war found us practically defenceless against the new enemy." He goes on to admit that a plan of campaign existed when he took over, two days after Rumania's declaration of war, but adds : " in view of our defective preparations, the plan of campaign which had been adopted had lost its original significance."[1]

In this he seems to do less than justice to his predecessor, for, as a matter of fact, the plan in its broad lines was immediately put into operation, and seems to have worked sufficiently well.

It is interesting to observe that the total forces actually facing or under orders for the Rumanian front at the end of August were as follows :—

Austrian.—4–5 weak divisions; 2 divisions and 1 cavalry division *en route;*

German.—$\frac{1}{3}$ division (the rest of the division on Salonika front); 4 divisions and 1 cavalry brigade *en route;*

Bulgaria.—2 strong divisions and $1\frac{1}{3}$ cavalry divisions, 2 strong divisions to come :

Turkish.—2 divisions *en route;*

giving a total of seven divisions and $1\frac{1}{3}$ cavalry divisions, rising by the middle of September to seventeen divisions and two to three cavalry divisions; against Rumania's twenty-three divisions, and two cavalry divisions, to be increased to twenty-five and three by Russian reinforcements moving to the Dobrudja.

Both had further possible reinforcements, the Rumanians from Russia, the enemy from Bulgaria, Turkey, Austria and Germany. But whilst the Rumanian general staff were in the position of the poor relation and had no say in the allotment of Russian resources, beyond commanding them if they arrived, the enemy operations were co-ordinated by the Germans who could effectively control their allies through possessing all the resources in money and material. As Rumania formed merely an extension of the Russian front, the Russian high command should theoretically have controlled the operations of the Rumanian Army. In practice such a solution was incompatible with Rumanian national sentiment and her distrust of Russia, and in the circumstances in which she entered the war could not be imposed upon her.

---

[1] "Out of my Life," p. 200.

II.

EVENTS UP TO 18TH SEPTEMBER. (*See* map number 3.)

Having now got a general view of the plans and resources of the two sides, we can proceed with the story.

On 28th August the covering troops of the Rumanian Armies, numbering above 135,000, advanced into Transylvania against very little opposition. In some places the Austrians carried out demolitions, notably of two large viaducts on the Ghimes pass railway—a serious matter for the Fourth Army—in others, positions were abandoned without a shot being fired.

By 9th September the outer wall had been scaled by the Fourth Army, and the enemy had retired to the inner bastion.

Meanwhile an event of far-reaching importance had occurred on the southern front, of which space permits only a very brief outline. Bulgaria waited only just long enough to complete her preparations, then on 1st September declared war, and immediately attacked, with a view to creating a diversion and weakening Rumania's Transylvanian offensive (*see* map number 3). The cavalry division, reinforced with machine gun cyclists and infantry, was despatched to give the impression of an advance northwards, cut the communication between Bazargic and Silistria and keep the Rumanian forces separated, the 12th Bulgarian division following a few days later. Under cover of this diversion, and also of a flank guard closer in, 31 battalions and 132 guns of the 1st and 4th Bulgarian divisions attacked Turtukai, garrisoned by the 17th division, a new formation of indifferent value, comprising some 19 battalions. The Bulgarians were comparatively well provided with heavy artillery, and with aeroplanes and captive balloons for observation of fire, which was opened on September 3rd.

The Rumanians, thoroughly alarmed for the safety of Bucharest, on 4th September moved the general reserve south by all available motor transport, the 10th division to Giurgevo, the 15th *viâ* Oltenita, whence its infantry crossed battalion by battalion to Turtukai, thus raising the garrison of the latter to 32 battalions and 156 guns. At the same time the 9th division, now under Russian command, was ordered to march south to the relief of Turtukai. Owing to faulty initial dispositions its commander could, however, collect only 5 battalions out of 16 for the purpose, and these were held up by the Bulgar covering force 10 miles away. An attack in flank by Bulgarian cavalry completed their discomfiture. On the 5th the Russian corps had arrived north of Bazargic, but effected nothing, for on 6th September the garrison of Turtukai surrendered, and 25,000 men, 100 guns, and 62 machine guns, with large warlike stores, passed into the enemy's hands. Only some 4,000 managed to effect their escape, either by swimming the Danube or slipping along the bank to Silistria. The enemy losses were under 8,000. One more had been added to the long list of fortresses which had failed to fulfil expectations; but it must be remembered that in practically every case they had been garrisoned by second or third-class troops. On the other side, one must remember Verdun.

Again, had the available Rumanian and Russian forces been concentrated, their flank or flanks resting on the protection afforded by Turtukai and Silistria, ready to act offensively, Bucharest and the Dobrudja would have been effectively protected, and the whole course of the campaign might have been altered. The lessons appear to be that fortresses must be held by good troops and that their value depends on their forming a pivot of manœuvre for an active field army.

The Rumanians, however, thoroughly frightened of fortresses after their experiences at Turtukai, were not prepared to make any attempt to utilise Silistria, and abandoned it on 9th August.

Mackensen then concentrated his forces and advanced northwards, the Russo-Rumanians opposing him retiring, after unsuccessful engagements, to the line of the old frontier, which line Mackensen successfully attacked on September 13th, 14th and 15th.

If the material losses at Turtukai were heavy, the moral effect was disastrous. Political circles in Bucharest were dumbfounded, and the whole plan of campaign was thrown into the melting pot, the popular apprehension being increased by a bombardment of Oltenita, which set fire to oil reservoirs, and seemed to presage an advance on Bucharest.

On 15th September a council of war was held, at which General Averescu, now appointed from command of the Second Army to that of the southern front, urged an offensive against Bulgaria; whilst General Presan, commanding the Fourth Army, who was making excellent progress in northern Transylvania, was equally insistent on adhering to the original plan.

Apparently no one could decide between the views of these outstanding personalities, and the worst possible conclusion was arrived at, viz., to do both.

In conformity with this compromise, the Dobrudja Army was to contain the 2nd, 5th, 9th, 12th, 15th (reformed) and 19th divisions, in addition to the 61st (Russian), the Serbian division, and a Russian cavalry division, and was to take the offensive southwards, whilst the 10th, 21st, 22nd, and 1st cavalry divisions, with the 16th and 18th already there, were to cross the Danube near Rahovo, seventy miles behind the Dobrudja front.

It will be seen from map number 3 that this plan effectually removed all the reserves on which the success of the Transylvanian offensive depended, the first and second armies between them losing five divisions and a cavalry division, whilst the general reserve also disappeared.

On the southern front it would result in the concentration of two masses, together totalling thirteen divisions and two cavalry divisions, seventy to ninety miles apart to deal with Mackensen's Army of only five to six divisions. It involved an opposed crossing of the Danube and heavy displacement of troops, with the loss of time thereby involved, when every day was of value in view of the probable movement of German reinforcements. It calls to mind our own east *versus* west controversy, which was partly responsible for the German break through in March, 1918.

Nor were the prospects of success improved by the fact that Averescu and Zaionchkovsky, commanding respectively the attacks across the Danube and down the Dobrudja, were independent of each other.

The results will appear in dealing with the Transylvanian offensive, to which we must now return.

III.

THE GERMAN COUNTEROFFENSIVE IN TRANSYLVANIA. (*See* map number 3.)

The Roumanian advance into Transylvania had proceeded methodically, if somewhat slowly, the enemy falling back and fighting only delaying actions, except in the Petroseni area, where he made a more determined resistance to cover his communications in the Maros valley. The advance was generally delayed, less by enemy resistance than by difficulties of communications, inexperience of commanders and staffs, and inability to prepare and push home attacks quickly, due partly to the deficiencies of equipment which have been mentioned.

Consequently, on 18th September, when Falkenhayn arrived on the scene at Deva to take over command of the Ninth Army, then in process of assembly, the Rumanian columns were still widely separated, and even where they were in touch, completely out of supporting distance of each other.

The situation, as it presented itself to Falkenhayn, was as follows (*See* map number 3):

The enemy was advancing slowly on a front of some two hundred miles in five main groups. With the forces at his disposal it was impossible to hold this front defensively; therefore, he must attack somewhere, and endeavour to seize the initiative. Obviously the enemy group which had crossed the Vulcan and Szurduk passes and captured Petroseni must be stopped, as it threatened the main railway communications most directly. This, however, had already been accomplished on 14th September by a counterattack of nine German and six Austrian battalions (including parts of the Alpine corps and 187th German division). Further east the 13th and 23rd Rumanian divisions on the outskirts of Sibiu (Hermannstadt) were being held with difficulty by some Austrian Honved and Landsturm units, stiffened with three German battalions.

Information was vague as to the Second Rumanian Army which had pushed forward into the wooded hills N.W. of Brasov (Kronstadt). In front of them were the 3rd German Cavalry Division (three regiments) and the Austrian 1st Cavalry Division (six regiments) connecting with the Austro-German forces opposing the Rumanian Second and Fourth Armies further east and north-east.

As regards reinforcements, the remaining two-thirds of the German Alpine corps was detraining near Sebesul Sasesc (Muhlbach). The 76th, also allotted to him, was moving towards Teius (Tovis). Further north the 89th German division had finished detraining at Maros Vasahely and the 72nd Austrian division was in process of doing so in the extreme left of the line.

The orders received by Falkenhayn from Hindenburg on 9th September, of which the following is a summary, will best show the general plans as conceived at G.H.Q. :—

"The task of the Ninth Army in conjunction with the First Army is to beat the enemy which has invaded Transylvania.

"The primary task of the First Army is to delay the enemy, and in conjunction with the Seventh Army (on the left of the First Army) to hold the Tarnava-Maros position, taking every opportunity of local counterattacks against the isolated portions of the advancing enemy.

"The Ninth Army will first drive back the enemy who have crossed the Szurduk pass, in order to be able to concentrate against the enemy near Hermannstadt (Sibiu) and envelop both his flanks.

"The right wing of the Ninth Army will hold back the enemy in the Orsova area.

"If forced to do so, the left wing of the Ninth Army will fall back in conjunction with the First Army in the general direction of Medias (Mediasch) and Dicso-Szt.-Marton."

Other detailed orders followed, to which Falkenhayn objected, and, after an exchange of telegrams, he was eventually given a free hand.

As a matter of fact he had already issued orders for the concentration of all available forces round Sibiu. The two brigades of the 187th division, and the one brigade of the Alpine corps near Petroseni (less one battalion and one battery each) were to move round at once by road and rail.

With the 76th division and 51st Austrian division, this would give him three German and one Austrian divisions against the two Rumanian divisions, and further he had a call on the 89th German division. It left only one indifferent Austrian brigade, stiffened by two German battalions and two batteries, to hold the Rumanians round Petroseni, and thus carried out in a high degree the principle of concentrating the maximum available force at the decisive time and place.

Orders for these moves were issued at midday on 19th September, but the troops from Petroseni had to make a long *détour* to reach Sibiu and the road and railway were in a very bad state. The Alpine corps could not begin its three days' turning movement into the mountains, which formed the basis of the plan of attack, until the 23rd and the combined attack must, therefore, necessarily be delayed until the 26th.

Much might happen in the intervening week if the Rumanians were enterprising, and Falkenhayn actually had some periods of acute anxiety.

On the 19th, detachments of the Rumanian Second Army made a movement down the Olt from Fogaras, unfortunately with such little determination that the German cavalry were able to stop them without much difficulty.

On 20th September the Austrians in the north began to give way, and it looked to Falkenhayn as if they might not hold long enough to enable his offensive to be delivered. It is difficult to agree with G.H.Q.'s conception (*vide* order quoted) that if the Austrians retired on his left, Falkenhayn could still carry out an envelopment of both Rumanian flanks at Sibiu (*see* map number 4), or even deliver his attack at all.

On the 22nd the Rumanians themselves assumed the offensive in force all along the front astride Sibiu, and their 13th division gained some success on the right wing against the Austrian 51st division and the cavalry, the latter being driven back from Glimboka northwards across the Haar. For a time it looked as if communication up the Olt with the Second Army would be opened, but here, as elsewhere, the Rumanians showed their weakness in attack and they made no effort to exploit their success on the 22nd and 23rd, nor, unfortunately, did the Second Army do anything to co-operate.

Now very anxious about his left flank, Falkenhayn asked the First Army to send the 89th division to Sighisoara (Schassburg), but in view of the critical situation of that army the request was not complied with. Eventually, by invoking the assistance of G.H.Q., Falkenhayn got it on the 27th, most unfortunately, as it turned out, for the Rumanians.

Meantime the latter had displayed commendable activity on the Petroseni front against the weak enemy forces left there to hold them. From the 23rd onwards they attacked strongly and on the 25th captured Petroseni and its valuable coal mines. Unfortunately they were not strong enough to seriously threaten Falkenhayn's communications in the Maros valley, and he did not allow this reverse to interfere with the arrangements for his main attack against the Red Tower pass, due to start the following morning.

Altogether Falkenhayn's situation during the period of preparation for the battle of Sibiu was not without its dangers. On his left there were grave doubts whether the Austrians would not go right back and leave him in the air and exposed to attack by the Second Rumanian Army. His right was also very far from secure. True he had the great advantage over his enemy that he was in easy communication with all parts of his front by telephone or motor-car; moreover he had good information from the air, which was denied to the enemy, and the population was quite as much pro-German as pro-Rumanian. His information was therefore much superior to that of the Rumanians, who were groping their way forward in the fog of war, their attacks apparently uncoordinated and their numerical superiority nullified by lack of fire power. Still, due credit must be given to him for sticking to his plan in the face of alarms and excursions on both his flanks.

The Rumanian forces, consisting of the 13th and 23rd divisions and six squadrons of Calarasi, were on a front of some ten to fifteen miles, with no reserves. Their orders were to take up a strong defensive position and await the advance of the other groups further east.

However, General Popovici decided to carry out the local offensive previously mentioned as alarming Falkenhayn, in order to improve the position and open up communication with the Second Army up the Olt valley.

The flank guard watching his right and maintaining communication with the Petroseni group consisted of one company of infantry, and although the concentration of enemy forces in front of him had been frequently reported by fleeing Rumanian inhabitants, no credence was apparently attached to this information until too late. Thus the march of the Alpine corps was quite unsuspected until the 24th; in fact the trap was sprung almost before he knew of its existence.

As soon as the danger was apparent, the G.O.C. of the First Army acted with promptitude, so far as his resources permitted. Part of the 20th division was hurried up from the Danube, whilst the Second Army was asked to send the nearest division down the Olt from Fogaras to attack the Germans in flank. To meet this request the 4th division had to be pulled out of the line, and passed behind the 3rd division, no free reserves being available in the army. Part of the 6th division was also withdrawn, but owing to the delay caused by marching across the communications of the 3rd division, arrived on the scene even later than the 4th division.

G.H.Q. do not appear to have taken any great interest in the matter, their attention being entirely fixed on their southern offensive, now about to mature.

The Battle of Sibiu (Hermannstadt), 25th–28th September, 1916.
(Map 4.)

Falkenhayn's original plan in conformity with G.H.Q. orders consisted of the envelopment of both wings of the Rumanian forces in front of the Red Tower pass. However, the Rumanian attack on the 22nd, which drove back his left, threatened, if continued, to interfere with the deployment of the 76th Reserve division which, moving round behind the cavalry, was to carry out the turning movement on the left. It was therefore modified to the following:—

> (a) The 187th, 51st Austrian, and 76th Reserve divisions in that order from right to left to attack astride Sibiu, main weight on the west of the town, objective Talmes ten to fifteen miles distant. This attack was to be supported by the three divisional artilleries, the field artillery of the Alpine corps (less one 4″ gun battery) and all the heavy artillery.

(b) The Alpine corps with its mountain artillery brigade, and two Austrian mountain batteries, to attack from the line Vrf Mare, Prezbe, Gyhan against the Red Tower pass, and cut the Rumanian line of retreat.

(c) The cavalry corps (one German and two Austrian brigades) had a dual *rôle* :—the first being to attack across the Olt, cut off any communication with the Rumanian Second Army, and, if possible, join hands with the Alpine corps, thus completing the circle. This comprehensive task was entrusted to three German cavalry regiments and a few guns. The second duty, viz. to stave off any attempts by the Second Rumanian Army to advance down the Olt valley, rested with the first Austrian cavalry division, which also had to maintain touch with the left of the First Army some twenty miles away to the east. It was supported by the 4" battery of the Alpine corps which played an important *rôle* in bluffing the Rumanian cavalry.

The plan was an extraordinarily bold one. To reach its position of deployment, the Alpine corps, minus all vehicles and equipped entirely with pack transport, started from Sina, some twenty miles west of Sibiu on September 22nd. It made its way over the mountains, in places well over 7,000 ft., through beech forest, then fir, and finally in the higher slopes through brushwood, and, after a march of nearly fifty miles, reached its allotted positions of deployment without encountering any enemy until quite close to the pass.

Falkenhayn was kept duly informed of its progress and knew that, so far, his plans were working well.

Not less ambitious perhaps, was the task allotted to the cavalry. Indeed it seemed only justifiable on the assumption that his main attack would forestall any intervention by Rumania's Second Army, or that the 89th division would be at hand in time to deal with the latter, for he had no other reserves. Both assumptions only just missed being falsified.

At daybreak on the 26th the German attack commenced. On the extreme right the Alpine corps met with immediate success, reaching the road through the Red Tower pass at several points. At Caneni the railway was blown up, and for a time the pass was closed. A Rumanian detachment trying to move into the pass was annihilated.

On the left a detachment of German cavalry with some guns crossed the Olt and deployed against the line Felek-F. Porumbak.

Rumanian cavalry advancing from the east along the foot of the mountains were stopped and driven back by the fire of the 4" battery.

The main attack, however, did not go quite so well. The 187th division on the right had by the evening carried the heights round Guraro and Poplaka, but the Rumanians still held D. Cioara and Balare. The 51st Austrian division, waiting for the 187th division to clear its front, did not advance; the 76th became involved in difficult country and did not even succeed in deploying for attack. In Falkenhayn's opinion the artillery was too much split up and badly handled. The appearance of the Rumanian cavalry on his left disquieted him, and he was far from satisfied with the general situation, especially as the only news from the Alpine corps was that it was being heavily counterattacked. He had no reserves, and therefore asked the First Army to send him the leading part of the 89th division. In consequence, one regiment and an artillery brigade were sent in tactical trains at once to Ocna Sibiiului (Salzburg), seven miles north of Sibiu.

Meantime the Rumanian efforts were mainly devoted to trying to open their line of retreat, and, thanks to the efforts of a regiment sent back from the front, and to units of the 20th division attacking from the south, these were partially successful; but Rumanian troops moving through the pass still had to run the gauntlet of artillery and machine gun fire.

27th September (second day of the battle).

The attack was renewed early on 27th, and with the help of the rear *échelon* of the Alpine corps the Oncesii hills were captured at an early hour. This led to the evacuation of the D. Cioara and Balare.

A well-executed Rumanian counterattack against the 51st Austrian division stopped the centre however, and by the evening the line ran from astride Disznod (Michelsburg) to just south of Selimbar (Schellenburg) and thence back to Kastenholz. The Rumanians were still fighting well, and the Germans could only get forward with concentrated artillery support.

The Alpine corps was holding its own with difficulty. During the day it was driven back from Veresterony and Caneni, and was hard pressed by attacks from the south against its positions west of the pass.

On the right, the Second Rumanian Army seemed at last to be in movement, strong bodies of cavalry advancing through Al. Bist, F. Bist, and F. Utfa, and disappearing into the woods. The last reserves of the cavalry corps were sent to oppose them at Kerzcisora, but no collision occurred.

Meantime the outflanking German cavalry were holding the Porumbak valley, thus closing the gap between the Olt and the mountains, whilst one squadron with machine guns had captured the heights of La Cetate and held its ground against counterattacks. This weak brigade was in fact holding two fronts facing respectively east and west some six miles apart, and was the only obstacle to a junction between the First and Second Rumanian Armies.

Falkenhayn was far from happy. The Rumanians still held a semicircular position covering the pass; the Alpine corps was still beyond supporting distance and was getting exhausted, and it was doubtful if the pass was really closed. The intervention of the Second Rumanian Army seemed imminent, and the big gap between his left and the right of the First Army was only watched by weak cavalry detachments. He decided to send a few infantry to help the cavalry, to put the regiment and artillery brigade of the 89th division, which had arrived from Ocna

Sibiiului (Salzburg), into the main attack and to order the remainder of that division to march from Sighisoara as rapidly as possible to Henndorf and Jacobsdorf, *i.e.*, behind the gap on his left, so as to arrive there on the following day (28th).

The Rumanian First Army still hoped that the Second Army would intervene, and, despite heavy bombing attacks from the air, maintained an intact front covering the entrance to the pass.

28th September (third day of the battle).

The German advance made good progress all along the line against weakening resistance, whilst the cavalry on the left wing gained ground across the Porumbako ravine. Further east, however, the weak covering detachment of cavalry facing east had been driven in during the night at Oprea-Kerzisora. Counterattacks had, however, temporarily checked the Rumanian advance, which actually was only made by weak infantry detachments. The 6th Austrian cavalry brigade connecting with the First Army reported that the right of the latter army south of Bekokten had been driven back towards the north-west, and that they themselves had been forced back into the hills north of the Olt as far west as Kerz. Falkenhayn urgently begged the First Army to hold a line in continuation of the Haar valley through Meschendorf.

By midday, however, the 89th division, after a forced march of 20 miles from Sighisoara, reached Jacobsdorf-Henndorf and proved the deciding factor.

Without waiting for orders its commander at once pushed his leading units forward, and their appearance on the flank of the Rumanian 4th division seems to have exerted as immediate and paralysing an effect as had similar Japanese action on Orlov's detachment at Liaoyang.

This must be attributed very largely to the want of air observation from which the Rumanians suffered throughout.

At nightfall the German centre was across the entrance to the pass just south of Talmesch.

The Alpine corps, much exhausted, had held its positions with difficulty against Rumanian counterattacks from the south. The cavalry connecting the German left with the Austrians were in such imminent danger of being driven off the field by the 4th Rumanian division, that Falkenhayn had to send up the infantry regiment and artillery brigade of the 89th division—allotted to the centre but not yet engaged—by march and motor to Nocrich (Leschkirch) and Agnita (Agnethlen).

The Fourth Rumanian Army in the north was advancing resolutely, but was too far away to effect the immediate issue. If, however, the Second Rumanian Army continued to push forward strongly there still seemed a chance that victory at the Red Tower pass might be snatched from his grasp. The capture of a Rumanian pilot bearing the following message, showed that such was the intention :—

To the Commander of the First Army.

"I have the honour to inform you that the Second Army advanced to within ten miles of your positions on evening 28th. We march between 4 and 5 a.m. on the 29th, bringing help and ammunition."

From Second Army.   Despatched 1.30 a.m. 29th September.

However, General Popovici, his men worn out and abandoning hope of any timely help from the Second Army, had already given the order to retreat. During the night 28th–29th the two divisions, with 2,000 vehicles, marched in close order back to Caneni through the ten-mile long pass which Falkenhayn fondly imagined to be firmly closed by the Alpine corps. As the road was still under machine gun fire in places this was a remarkable performance, particularly on the part of the artillery, who drew the enemy's fire with civilian waggons, and then galloped batteries past the danger points.

Thus the "bag" fell far short of what Falkenhayn had anticipated, for he only collected 3,000 prisoners, 13 guns, 2 aeroplanes and 70 lorries.

Strategically, however, the victory was decisive. It showed that the imposing façade of the Rumanian offensive into Transylvania was a mere shell, with nothing behind it; it robbed them of the initiative on the northern front, and spelt the failure of the southern offensive before it had even started.

The tactical mistakes of General Popovici which led to his supercession are obvious: the failure to watch his left flank, the wide extension of front in a too forward position without any adequate reserve. These, however, were minor errors in comparison with the faulty strategy of the high command, which should never have placed him in such a position. A similar disaster, if not to him, was bound to occur in the circumstances, given an energetic and capable adversary such as Falkenhayn. That the latter was lucky does not detract from the merit of his strategical insight and the boldness with which he initiated and carried out his plan; but he must have failed had any of the divisions standing idle opposite Rahovo been where they should have been according to the original Rumanian plan.

Let us see what these divisions actually accomplished.

IV.

The Rumanian Offensive in the Dobrudja and the Crossing of the Danube at Rahovo.

Mackensen, continuing his offensive in the Dobrudja, had attacked the Rumanian position Tuzla-Cobadin-Rosova unsuccessfully from 16th September to the 19th. The latter, reinforced by the 115th Russian division, then commenced a counteroffensive, as the result of which the enemy was forced to withdraw a short distance, but as a combined operation with the crossing of the Danube at Rahovo the venture completely miscarried.

The latter operation was commenced by the 10th and 21st divisions on the evening of October 1st, *i.e.*, just after the Sibiu (Hermannstadt) defeat. In the face of considerable artillery fire and bombing from aircraft, which caused heavy loss, a bridgehead was formed and pushed out towards Turtukai and Ruscuk.

The following day the rain came down in torrents and the Danube rose; enemy monitors appeared and broke through the Rumanian defensive minefield, incendiary mines drifted down on the pontoon bridge, which was also bombed from the air, and between them all it was broken on 2nd October.

Moreover, the news from Transylvania which threatened the security of Bucharest from the north, necessitated the reinforcement of that front. Consequently the withdrawal of the troops which had crossed was commenced under great difficulties, but was successfully accomplished, with the exception of a small rearguard, which was practically annihilated on 5th October.

Hindenburg's comment on the Rahovo enterprise was not far wide of the mark :—[1]

> "A fine plan on paper! Whether it was a Rumanian inspiration or that of one of her allies is still unknown, even to-day. After the experiences which the Rumanians had had of us before the day of the Rahovo interlude, I regarded the enterprise as more than bold, and not only thought to myself, but said openly ' these troops will all be caught.' "

That the last remark was falsified was due perhaps to the floods which may have proved a blessing in disguise, as stopping the operation before it had gone too far to withdraw.

It is interesting to note that whilst the Rumanian armies had suffered decisive defeats on both northern and southern fronts owing to lack of troops at the decisive point, the 10th, 16th, 18th, 21st and 22nd divisions had played no useful part

Towards producing this unfortunate result the abortive Rahovo enterprise had completed the work which Turtukai had begun.

The situation was aptly described by a distinguished British officer on 9th October, as follows :—[2]

> "On Rumania's entry into the war I drew attention to her faulty dispositions and predicted defeat in detail. This is what has taken place, and will continue to take place, until a definite plan is adopted and adhered to. I have, up to the present, been unable to trace any such plan. Including the Russian-Serbian divisions, Rumania possesses superiority over all enemy forces opposing her, and she should decide definitely where she will take the offensive and where she will stand on the defensive."

---

[1] "Out of my Life," p. 201. [2] General Sir William Robertson.

It must be added, however, that a more intimate knowledge of the Rumanian army and of the Russian divisions might have led him to modify his opinion as to the possibility of the former taking the offensive with any chance of success at this stage without stronger Russian backing.

V.

The Battles of Sinca (Geisterwald) and Brasov (Kronstadt).
(*See* map number 5.)

As a result of the defeat at Sibiu the First and Second Rumanian Armies were at first directed to remain on the defensive pending the development of the Rahovo enterprise. With this object the Second Army, attacking in two directions and its three divisions much dispersed, was ordered to concentrate towards Brasov, the idea being to form a firm pivot so as to permit the Fourth Army to continue its successful advance so soon as the necessary reinforcements were available. It was thus hoped to retain some initiative in Transylvania. It was quickly seen, however, that the Rahovo offensive was not going to meet with sufficient success to affect the situation generally, and fears for the city of Bucharest compelled the withdrawal of the 21st and 22nd divisions.

For the moment the Rumanian primary concern was to secure the position of the Second Army, otherwise the Fourth Army would be in danger of isolation, its right flank also being in the air owing to the complete inactivity of the Russians.

The Rumanians appear to have oscillated for some days between the above plan and a complete abandonment of Transylvania, until the battle of Brasov settled the question definitely for them.

The German Plan.

With the retirement of the bulk of the First Rumanian Army across the frontier, its Petroseni detachment was left in the air, and ceased to affect the general situation. The German general staff had, therefore, the choice before them of an immediate advance into Wallachia in pursuit of the First Army or to turn against the Rumanian Second Army.

The former alternative does not appear to have been seriously considered by Hindenburg, presumably because the pressure exerted by the Fourth Rumanian Army (and to a lesser extent by the Second Army) was already threatening the railheads in the Maros and the two Tarnava valleys, and therefore the main communications of the Austro-Germans in Transylvania. (*See* map number 3.)

In the general defence of the Rumanian frontier the Fourth Army was thus continuing to pull its weight, and apparently it was not yet clear to the Germans that, both tactically and strategically, the initiative had passed to them. No doubt the hope of marching from Brasov direct on Bucharest was at the back of Hindenburg's mind, and Mackensen was not yet ready to cross the Danube.

Actually, orders for a subsequent concentric attack on Brasov and the Second Rumanian Army had been issued by Hindenburg on 24th September, *i.e.*, before the commencement of the battle of Sibiu.

Still, it is an interesting strategic question to consider what might have been the effect on Rumanian nerves of a German irruption into Wallachia at the end of September—an operation which was only effected after much fighting and loss two months later.

Might it not have been an even more certain method of clearing Transylvania than an attack on the Second Army?

The plan actually adopted was by a rapid advance of the Ninth Army up the Olt to seize the passes in rear of the Second Rumanian Army, round up the latter, and then march direct on Bucharest.

It is not proposed to follow the operations in any great detail as they led to no decisive result, but merely to give a general outline.

Falkenhayn's original intention was to relieve the Alpine corps by the 51st Austrian division, with a view to using that *corps d'élite* for another outflanking movement through the mountains against the communications of the Second Army.

Successful attacks by the latter, however, on the 29th, which penetrated as far as the Haar, threatened to separate him from the Austrians on his left, and caused such alarm and despondency amongst the latter that he could not wait to relieve the Alpine corps nor to collect the detachments of his other three divisions which were following the 13th and 23rd Rumanian divisions through the Red Tower pass.

With his three divisions (76th reserve, 51st Austrian, 187th) covered by the cavalry, Falkenhayn marched up the Olt. The Austrian Army on his left was placed under his operational control and its right corps (89th German and 71st Austrian divisions) was to attack Brasov from the north. This would tend to draw that corps away from the commander of the First Austrian Army, operating against the Fourth Rumanian Army further north.

As the country round Brasov was considered unsuitable for cavalry, the bulk of the latter was to move round north of it to fill the gap, and cut the passes behind the Fourth Rumanian Army.

The plan aimed at no less than the encircling of both the Second and Fourth Armies, their defeat west of the frontier, and the opening of the latter on a wide front for an advance on Bucharest.

The Rumanian 4th division retiring in front of the Germans—who were delayed by bad weather—occupied a position on the western edge of the Geisterwald running through Comana–Persiani and thence along the Sinca.[1]

Here it was reinforced by a brigade of all arms of the 6th division.

---

[1] The name given to the ensuing battle is the battle of Sinca by the Rumanians, and the battle of the Geisterwald by the Germans.

The Germans attacked on the morning of 5th October, and finding that the 51st (Austrian) division and 76th reserve division were confronted by strong positions, the 187th was directed to turn the Rumanian right in the direction of Grid. A combined attack by all three divisions eventually ejected the Rumanians, despite several gallant counterattacks, which were shattered by the concentrated fire of the German artillery.

By the afternoon the Rumanians were retreating into the wooded hills, leaving 43 guns in the enemy's hands, including all those belonging to the 6th division.

The Battle of Brasov (Kronstadt). (October 7th–8th.)

His success on 5th October encouraged Falkenhayn in the belief that the Second Rumanian Army might be annihilated by an encircling movement from both flanks, although obviously this would be rendered difficult by the fact that several passes led out of the Brasov basin.

In pursuance of this plan the First Austrian Army on his left was to follow the Fourth Rumanian Army with weak detachments only, since no great success could be anticipated in the narrow valleys through which the latter was retiring.

The cavalry corps, so far as the state of its horses permitted, was to operate against its flank with the dual object, if possible, of cutting its communications and preventing it from giving any assistance to the Second Army.

Under this screen the 89th and 71st (Austrian) divisions were to make a sweep and come in against Brasov from the north and north-west.

The XXXIX. corps (76th Reserve, 51st (Austrian), and 187th divisions) was to attack in an easterly direction so as to envelop the town from the south, the enveloping nature of the attack being emphasised by the despatch of specially selected detachments to seize the Predeal pass and so cut the main Rumanian line of communication. The 8th Austrian mountain brigade from the Izonzo, which had detrained at Sibiu on the 5th, was ordered to push forward along the crest of the frontier range to the Königstein with a similar object.

The Rumanians had originally intended to evacuate Brasov and fall back to the frontier fortifications. They had actually commenced the retirement on the night 6th/7th when the arrival of the 21st and 22nd divisions at Predeal and Campulung caused them to change their mind. The troops were countermarched and a position was occupied by the 3rd, 4th, and 6th divisions, its right on the Olt near Harman, thence in front of Brasov to Zernesti. On the extreme right towards Sepsi St. George was a brigade of the 6th division, and further north a detachment from the 2nd cavalry division with some infantry from the Fourth Army.

The arrival of the leading brigade of the 22nd division from near Campulung on the 7th enabled the left to be extended just in time.

The German attack opened on the 7th October, and the 187th and 51st Austrian divisions made good progress, as the position was not fully occupied by the Rumanians. Harman and Sampietru were taken, but in the afternoon Rumanian counterattacks drove the Germans back and re-established the position.

Falkenhayn states that these counterattacks caused him no anxiety, as the further the Rumanian right wing advanced, the more effective would be the counterattack of the 89th and 71st (Austrian) divisions when it developed. Their movement had, however, been delayed by the natural difficulties of the country and by the poor marching powers of the 89th division.

On the German right but little progress had been made, thanks to the arrival of the leading brigade of the 22nd division, which occupied the D. Muscelului and defeated all efforts to eject or outflank it.

October 8th. Second Day of the Battle of Brasov.

During the night a brigade of the 21st Rumanian division, whose artillery was already in action, had been put into the line in the centre. The Germans at first fought their way forward, but in the afternoon the Rumanians passed to the offensive in the centre and right. The 6th division attacking from the north-east threatened to roll up the German left, which was also attacked frontally by the 3rd division. The situation of the 187th division became far from pleasant, and the 89th division was told to hasten its movements. It did not, however, succeed in intervening effectually owing to weariness, bad reconnaissance and broken bridges, and at nightfall its head was only entering Bot. The 71st (Austrian) division was still completely out of the hunt.

Further north the so-called 3rd German cavalry division (three regiments) was easily held by the Rumanian mixed detachments from the Fourth Army, whilst the 1st Austrian cavalry division had been quite unsuccessful in its attempts to interfere with the retirement of the Fourth Army.

Against the Rumanian left, however, the attack had made great progress, and at one period it looked as if the Rumanian main line of retreat would be cut, as at the Red Tower pass.

A considerable concentration of artillery had been effected against the Rumanian positions on D. Muscelului, and as soon as it opened fire the defence melted away.

The Germans pursuing, captured the heights on either side of the Bran pass, and the way to Campulung seemed open. Orders were sent to the 8th mountain brigade to bear to the right and make for the Bran Pass road further down the mountains behind the Rumanians. A detachment of two battalions with some artillery was also despatched to cut the Predeal pass. The Rumanians, remembering the Alpine corps at Sibiu, were not, however, to be caught twice in the same way, and a brigade of the 21st division sent up from Predeal made short work of the two battalions and re-occupied the Postovar, thus covering their communications.

October 9th.

Falkenhayn's orders for the 9th included a continuation of the attack, and the despatch of the 3rd German cavalry division towards the Oituz pass.

G.H.Q.'s ideas were even more ambitious, as at this juncture they issued orders to Falkenhayn to seize the passes round Brasov and also to despatch infantry and cavalry to Onesti in the Trotus valley, with the dual object of cutting the line of communication of the Fourth Army and of preventing the arrival of any Russian reinforcements by the Trotus valley railway.[1]

It would appear that the Germans might have been better advised to have made certain of completing one operation before initiating another, for on the night of the 8th/9th the Rumanians effected their retirement to positions covering the passes leading from the Brasov basin, before the enveloping attack of the 89th and 71st Austrian divisions had started. Nor did the 8th Austrian mountain brigade get up in time to take any part in the battle.

Falkenhayn failed, therefore, in his attempt to effect a concentration of all his forces on the battlefield, and had the Rumanian Army possessed the power to strike a powerful blow quickly, their counterattack on the 8th might have dealt hardly with him, whilst nearly half his forces were absent from the battlefield. As it was, it resulted in heavy Rumanian casualties, incommensurate, perhaps, with the results obtained.

Still, though the Rumanians had suffered heavily both in men and material, they had slipped out of the net, after effecting the evacuation of most of the stores at Brasov and seeing the Fourth Army safely withdrawn. Moreover, they still blocked the passes leading to Bucharest, and the hardest part of Falkenhayn's task lay before him.

Up to this point his operations had been uniformly successful. In less than a month he had succeeded in throwing a numerically superior enemy on to the defensive and had practically cleared Transylvania.

That this result was due largely to superiority in communications, mobility and every technical adjunct to modern warfare is undeniable. Still, the operations of the Ninth German Army form a model of how a mountain range may be defended, just as the Rumanian plan emphasises by its failure the danger of concentrating isolated columns forward in the presence of an enterprising and mobile enemy.

---

[1] The 71st division was eventually ordered to follow the 1st Austrian cavalry division to carry out this task.

APPENDIX A.

RUMANIAN EFFECTIVES MOBILISED OR MOBILISABLE ON THE DECLARATION OF WAR IN AUGUST, 1916.

		Officers.	Other Ranks.
A. (a) Field Army		13,561	562,847
(b) L. of C. troops for Field Army		1,707	59,051
Total Field Army		15,268	621,898
B. Depôts		4,575	191,869
C. Men excepted on mobilisation or put back, but available if required :—			
(a) Trained		—	82,993
(b) Exempted or put back		—	102,117
(c) Temporarily unfit, but called up later		—	25,900
(d) Contingent of 1917 (actually joined in Oct.)		—	55,545
		—	266,555
Grand Total		19,843	1,080,313

Categories A and B were mobilised at the commencement.

Category C was incorporated in the field army during 1916 and the following winter, to replace casualties.

Thus the total mobilised for the field army amounted to 1,080,313.

Men over 42 and between 19 and 21 years of age who were employed in non-combatant duties are not included in the above total.

The 1918–1919 classes were also called up in the winter of 1916–1917 to the number of 110,000.

(To be continued.)

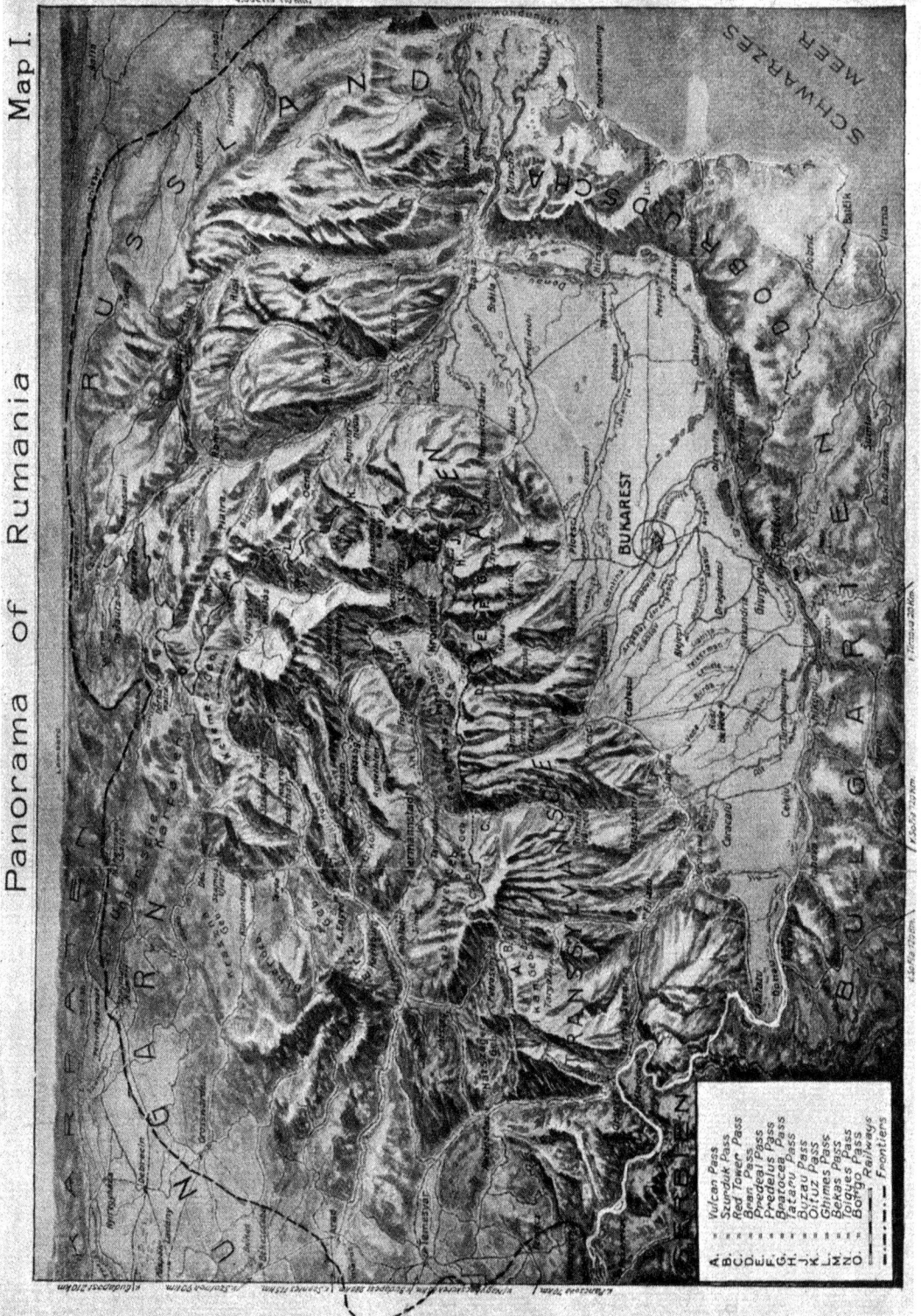

Map I. Panorama of Rumania

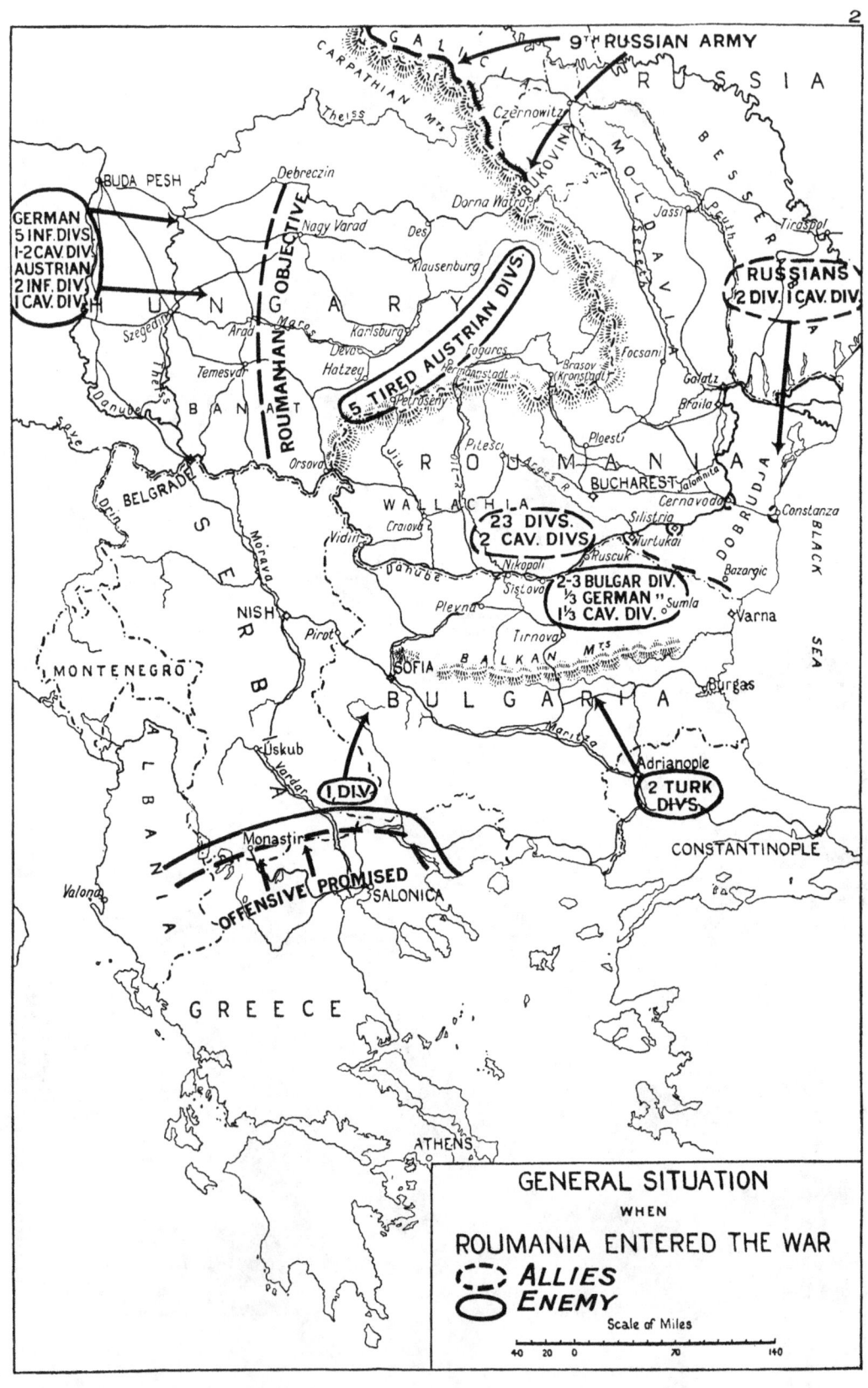

GENERAL MAP OF RUMANIA

SHOWING RUMANIAN STRATEGIC DEPLOYMENT AND SITUATION ON SEPT 18TH

Legend:
- ③ INITIAL POSITION OF RUMANIAN 3RD DIV. ACCORDING TO PLAN OF STRATEGIC DEPLOYMENT
- 3 POSITION OF 3RD DIV. ON 18TH SEPT.
- AUSTRO-GERMAN POSITIONS ON 18TH SEPT. 72(A)D. MEANS 72ND AUSTRIAN DIV.
- → BULGARIAN OPENING MOVES

Passes:
- A — Iron Gates
- B — Vulcan Pass
- C — Szurduk Pass
- D — Red Tower Pass (Rother Turm)
- E — Bran Pass (Törzburg)
- F — Predeal Pass (Tömös)
- G — Predelus Pass (Altschanz)
- H — Brašovča Pass (Tartarang)
- J — Tatáru Pass (Tatahavas)
- K — Buzau Pass (Bodza)
- L — Oitoz Pass
- M — Ghimes Pass
- N — Bekas Pass
- O — Tölgyes Pass

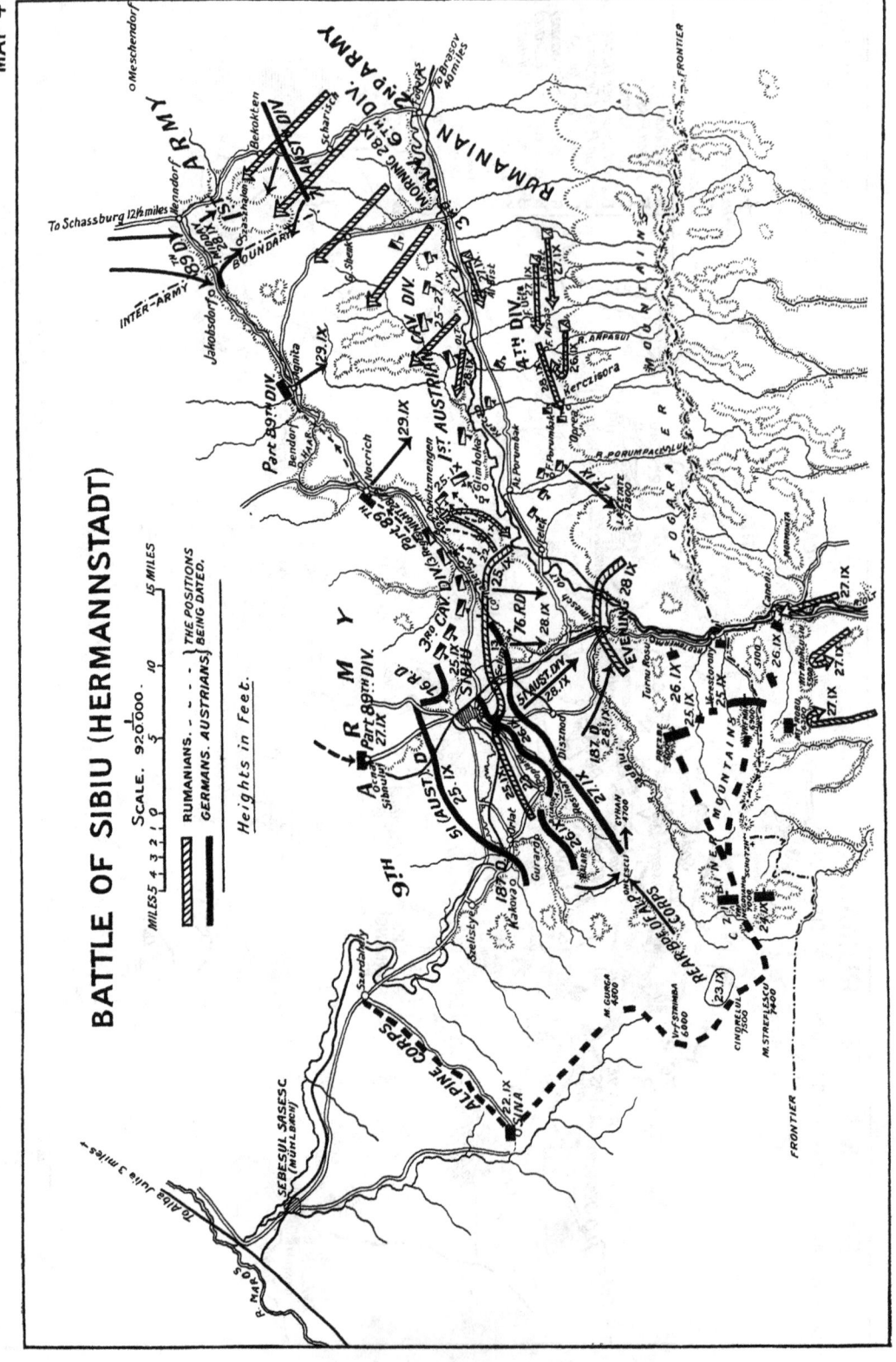

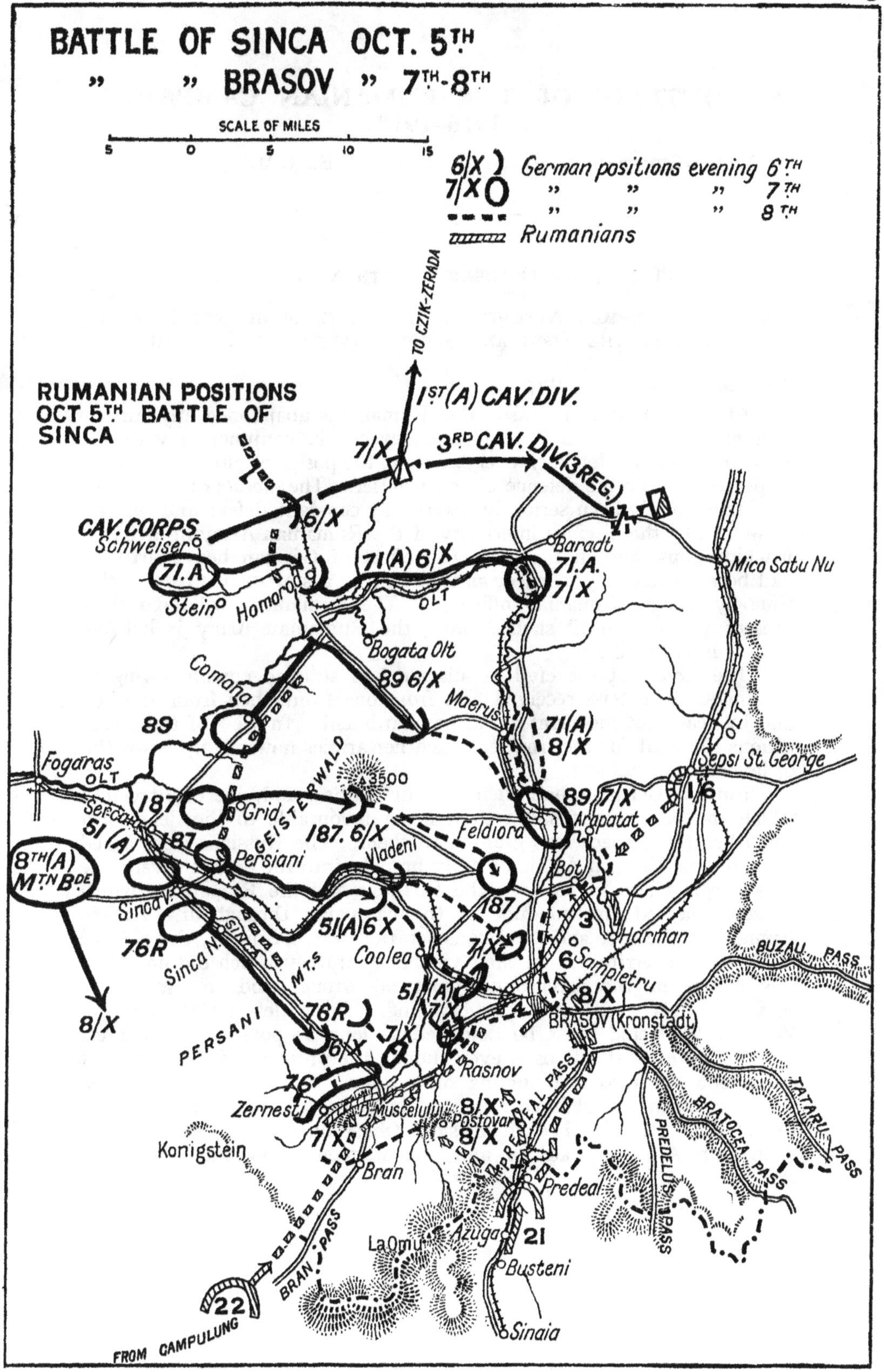
BATTLE OF SINCA OCT. 5TH
" " BRASOV " 7TH-8TH
SCALE OF MILES
5 0 5 10 15
6/X German positions evening 6TH
7/X " " " 7TH
" " " 8TH
Rumanians
RUMANIAN POSITIONS OCT 5TH BATTLE OF SINCA
TO CZIK-ZERADA
1ST(A) CAV. DIV.
3RD CAV. DIV. (3 REG.)
7/X
6/X
CAV. CORPS
Schweiser
71.A
Stein
Homorod
71(A) 6/X
OLT
71.A. 7/X
Baradt
Mico Satu Nu
Bogata Olt
Comana
89 6/X
Maerus
71(A) 8/X
89
Fogaras
OLT
3500
GEISTERWALD
187
Grid
Sercaia
51(A)
Persiani
187. 6/X
Feldiora
89 7/X
Arapatat
Sepsi St. George
1/6
8TH(A) MTN BDE
Vladeni
Bot
Sinca V.
51(A) 6 X
187
76R
Sinca N.
SINCA
7/X
3
Harman
Coolea
6
Sampietru
BUZAU PASS
51(A) 7/X
8/X
8/X
PERSANI MTS
76R
7/X
4
BRASOV (Kronstadt)
6/X
Rasnov
76
PREDEAL PASS
TATARU PASS
Zernesti
D. Muscelului
8/X
Postovar
8/X
BRATOCEA PASS
7/X
Konigstein
Bran
PREDELUS PASS
Predeal
BRAN PASS
Azuga
21
LaOmu
Busteni
22
FROM CAMPULUNG
Sinaia

AN OUTLINE OF THE RUMANIAN CAMPAIGN, 1916–1918.

By Major-General W. M. St. G. Kirke, C.B., C.M.G., D.S.O., *p.s.c.*

PART II. (30th October to 25th November, 1916).

The Austro-German Attempts to break through into Rumania, including the First and Second Battles of Targujiu.

The Rumanian plan. (Map 6.)

After the battle of Brasov the Rumanians abandoned any further idea of an offensive in Transylvania, except in conjunction with the Russians, and they fell back everywhere to the positions already prepared in peace time for the defence of the frontier. The *morale* of the troops had undoubtedly been seriously lowered by constant defeat and retreat, as well as by the obvious inferiority of the Rumanian Army in artillery, machine guns, and in the air. The effect of German heavy artillery had been particularly marked, as is shown by a statement made at this time by a high Rumanian officer :—" The Rumanians will hold their present positions until shelled out; the Rumanian Army is helpless against heavy artillery."

The *morale* of the civil population had suffered equally owing to continuous bad news received first from one front, then from another, and by reason of incessant aerial bombardment. In view of these conditions the fight for the frontier which her armies now put up is worthy of favourable comment.

But the Germans had their own difficulties, and, the country into which the Rumanians had retired being favourable to the defence, a small breathing space was granted to them. The Russians were asked for help, and General Alexieff's reply brought into the open a divergence of strategic views as between the Russians and the Rumanians which gravely affected the conduct of the campaign throughout. To the Rumanians the first and vital consideration was, naturally, the defence of Rumanian territory. In their view any strategy which did not place this object in the foreground must be wrong, and to secure it they were prepared to risk everything. The indefensible salient of Western Wallachia must be defended as long as possible : Bucharest must be covered at all costs, even though the presence of the enemy at Cernavoda involved the holding of a salient hardly less pronounced. No Government could have remained in power which did not take up this standpoint. The French Mission, whose duty it was to assist the Rumanian Army by advice and encouragement—at this time they possessed no other means of assisting Rumania—strongly supported that view.

But to the Russians the picture appeared quite otherwise. Looking at their long line from the Baltic to the Black Sea as a whole, and the Rumanian Army as merely a unit in it, Rumania appeared as a salient which practically doubled the length of the Russian front. So long as they were acting offensively this was no great disadvantage, since it tended to separate and disperse the enemy forces. If, however, they were definitely thrown on to the defensive, it would be sound strategy to shorten the front to be defended as much as possible. A retirement to the line of the Sereth down to Galatz and thence along the Danube to the sea would reduce it by over 600 miles. In the matter of withdrawals the Russians were accustomed to think large. To them the abandonment of a few thousand square miles of their own country—still less of someone else's—meant nothing very much. What to the Rumanians seemed inconceivable perfidy had always proved one of the strongest cards in Russian strategy.

Even before the necessity had actually arisen, highly-placed Russians, who had preceded the arrival of Russian forces in Rumania, were foolish enough to discuss it openly, and the effect may well be imagined. Hence, doubtless, arose accusations that the Russians never had any intention of assisting in the defence of Rumania; that her overthrow, indeed, would be by no means unwelcome to them. It has even been stated that Baron Sturmer, the Russian Prime Minister, intended to make friends with Germany by a partition of Rumania's dead body. It would be a bold man who would venture to make a categorical statement on any subject connected with Russian diplomacy. Such may have been his intention, but it seems safe to assert that he could not have carried it out so long as the Czar was on the throne.

Alexieff's reply to the Rumanian request for help had more regard for Rumanian susceptibilities than to suggest a retirement to the Sereth, but was sufficiently unpalatable. He proposed that a line of defence should be taken up running from Dorna Vatra in the northern corner of Rumania *via* Czik Czerada–Brasov–Bucharest to Constanza. From the flanks of this line Russian offensives were to be directed into northern Transylvania and the Dobrudja respectively. This plan meant the voluntary abandonment of Western Wallachia, the richest part of Rumania, and, needless to say, was entirely inacceptable to the Rumanian Government. We who held the costly Ypres salient throughout the war for far less solid reasons may fully appreciate their sentiments. A less drastic suggestion put forward by the British C.I.G.S., that a retirement to the line of the Olt was advisable in view of the exposed and isolated positions of the Jiu and Cerna detachments, was equally inacceptable to M. Bratiano, though advocated also by General Presan. The Rumanians thus adhered to their plan of defending the whole of their long frontier, hoping that the promised Russian offensives would soon materialise to relieve pressure, whilst the Russians proceeded with their preparations for offensives in northern Transylvania and the Dobrudja, hoping that the Rumanians would hold in the centre, yet feeling not very confident about it, nor very concerned if they failed. Obviously a supreme command was very badly needed.

The German plan.

Falkenhayn had hoped that he might be able to follow on the heels of the retreating Rumanians and force the passes leading to Bucharest. The timely retirement of the Second Army and the reinforcements which the Rumanians had brought, and were still bringing up, rendered this a far more difficult task than he had anticipated. Moreover, he was faced by much the same difficulties which the Rumanians had experienced in their initial advance, increasing with every mile which he penetrated into the mountains. Maintenance of the troops on the different roads was not easy, and railheads were still six marches away at Sibiu (Hermannstadt) and Sighisoara (Schassburg); it was, consequently, impossible to concentrate any large force on any one road without delay and surrendering the factor of surprise; deployment off the roads was difficult, and the heavy artillery, on which he particularly relied, was much handicapped in consequence.

He decided, in view of the difficulties mentioned above, to attack everywhere along the 150 miles of Transylvanian frontier from the Szurduk to the Buzau Pass inclusive, in the hopes of finding a weak spot and then of exploiting it with the fresh divisions now under orders for Transylvania. He relied on surprise and the loss of resisting power of the Rumanians rather than on weight in any one attack. If a break in the defences could be made, the shape of the frontier and the superiority of the Transylvanian railway system, specially designed for the invasion of Rumania, would give him a great advantage over the Rumanians, even though these latter might locally be operating on interior lines.

If Falkenhayn's plan involved dispersion as opposed to concentration, G.H.Q.'s ideas tended even farther in the same direction. Under Hindenburg's instructions, the First and Ninth armies were to attack in eccentric directions :—

    (*a*) towards Onesti, *i.e.*, to the N.E.;
    (*b*) a main attack towards Bucharest, *i.e.*, to the S.E.;
    (*c*) towards Curtea d'Arges, *i.e.*, to the S. and S.W.

Falkenhayn sarcastically remarks that this may have looked a very nice plan on a conference table at G.H.Q. in Pless, where they seemed obsessed by the idea of a Russo-Rumanian counter-attack in North Transylvania,[1] but it took no account of the exhausted condition of his troops, nor of their losses, which in many units had reduced effectives by 50 per cent. He might have added that, like his own plan, it underestimated the value of the enemy. However, he complied to a certain

---

[1] NOTE.—The German information concerning what was passing through the minds of the Russian High Command seems to have been remarkably accurate.

extent by sending Von Schmettow's Cavalry Corps (three brigades), followed by the 71st Division, towards the Oituz Pass, and then directed his remaining columns to push forward from the Brasov basin—

(1) the 89th Division against the Buzau Pass;

(2) the 51st Austrian and 187th Divisions against the Predeal (Tomos) and Predelus (Altschantz) Passes;

(3) the 76th Division and 8th Austrian Mountain Brigade to exploit their success towards Campulung;

(4) the Alpine Corps, with the 2nd and 10th Austrian Mountain Bdes., now arriving, to force a passage down the Olt valley.

We shall see what happened to the enterprise towards the Oituz Pass when dealing with the operations of the Fourth Rumanian Army. As regards the remainder, the advance on the Buzau and Predeal Passes could progress but slowly in the face of increasing resistance and corresponding losses, the country favouring the Rumanians, who, according to Falkenhayn, obtained excellent information from the inhabitants and were falling back on to more or less prepared positions. Nor was the advance towards Campulung much more fortunate in spite of an initial success at Rucar due to the arrival of the 8th Austrian Mountain Brigade behind the Rumanians, who once again were caught napping by the enemy's superior enterprise in the utilisation of mountain paths. By the 13th October the Rumanians were everywhere back to, or over, their frontier, but the idea of brushing them quickly aside had not materialised.

G.H.Q., however, still adhered to its strategic conception and now regrouped the Ninth, First and Seventh armies under the Archduke Charles, to Falkenhayn's great annoyance. Army Group orders to the latter were to the following effect—

"Our task is to complete the destruction of the enemy forces opposed to us before they can be reinforced.

"Responsibility for effecting this object rests primarily with you.

"The main Rumanian Armies are to be sought out in the direction of Bucharest, and that will be the general direction of your attack.

"The right wing of your army—the reinforced Alpine Corps—will be directed on Curtea d'Arges, whilst the troops in the Petroseni and Orsova areas will take every opportunity of advancing on Craiova.

"The choice of directing your main attack on Campulung, Targoviste, or Ploesti is left to you, in accordance with where you succeed in penetrating the frontier defences. The strong cavalry reinforcements shortly arriving (6th and 7th Cavalry Divisions) will enable you not only to guard your left flank in the direction of Buzau, but also to separate the enemy groups by pushing forward into the lower Sereth valley."

Falkenhayn, as usual, objected; G.H.Q. was appealed to and issued fresh directions. Falkenhayn considered them just as bad, on the grounds that he had insufficient force for an advance on Bucharest and wanted the cavalry on the other flank to that indicated by the Group Command. Moreover, he entirely disapproved of the enterprise towards Onesti, because it tended to divert reinforcements from his own army. Nevertheless he obeyed orders to the extent of maintaining pressure on the Brasov group of passes, and continued his efforts to debouch from Dragoslavele into the more open country round Campulung. At the same time he went on with his preparations for attacking down the Olt. This, if successful, would, in conjunction with a converging attack through Campulung, give him the vital junction of Pitesti, and so cut all railway communications with Western Wallachia. This again should tend to draw Rumanian reinforcements away from the Brasov group of passes and thereby facilitate the main task allotted to him, viz., a direct advance through them on Bucharest.

First Battle of the Olt, 15th–21st October. (Map. 6).

The battle of the Olt opened on the 15th October, the plan comprising wide outflanking attacks over the mountains by the 10th Austrian Mountain Brigade on the right, and the newly arrived 2nd Austrian Mountain Brigade on the left, whilst the Alpine Corps advanced astride the main Olt road on a front of about eight miles. Supply was the main difficulty as the flanking columns moved over mountain paths involving some stiff climbing. It is not proposed to follow this battle in detail, as it developed into a "slogging match." By the evening of the 15th the attack had made good progress, but on the 18th the Rumanians commenced a series of counterattacks and the weather turned suddenly cold. Paths became icebound and slippery, and supply of food and ammunition over the mountains increasingly difficult for the Germans, though every able-bodied man and woman of the inhabitants was forcibly enlisted by the Germans for compulsory transport labour.

The Austro-Germans struggled on and by the 21st had got within six miles of Ramnicu-Valcea, but they had shot their bolt and could make no further headway. Then, in the face of repeated counterattacks and running short of ammunition, they were forced back 12 to 15 miles, having suffered considerable losses. The operation had totally miscarried. On the other hand, the fact that they remained in possession of a somewhat more forward line than before, would assist a second attempt; moreover, the Rumanian casualties had been very heavy.

The spell of cold weather had had an equally unfavourable effect on German operations south of Brasov, the Rumanians contesting strongly any enemy attempts to advance, and severely handling some of the isolated columns.

On the 21st October, Falkenhayn reported to G.H.Q. in the following sense :—

" The bad weather and the lateness of the season makes it questionable whether it is worth while to repeat similar attempts.

Short of proper equipment for the individual soldier, of mountain artillery and pack transport, attacks over frozen or snow-covered hills against prepared positions backed by adequate communications have little hope of success. On the other hand, the inhabitants say that winter proper has not yet arrived, etc., etc."

This tale of woe naturally led up to a request for reinforcements. In the meantime he determined to make another attempt to break through, this time viâ the Vulcan and Szurduk passes, down the Jiu valley. As it resulted in one of the most interesting battles of the war, it will now be described in some detail.

The First Battle of Targujiu, Oct. 23rd–30th. (Map 7).

The troops to be employed for a break through over the Vulcan and Szurduk Passes were the 301st Division (comprising the 144th Austrian Brigade, 2 Batteries and 2 Cyclist Battalions), a fresh Division (the 11th Bavarian), and the 6th German Cavalry Division (3 Brigades). The 7th German Cavalry Division and two fresh Infantry Divisions were under orders and would be available to exploit the expected success.

The Rumanians, who were holding the main crest of the frontier range, consisted of some 13 battalions and 7 batteries. The Austro-German superiority was, therefore, assured provided the defence were not reinforced. Attacks on the Orsova front were designed to prevent this; moreover it was hoped that the attack of the Alpine Corps down the Olt valley would have tended to draw troops from the Jiu and so further weaken the defence. Neither assumption proved correct. The Szurduk Pass, the cleft formed by the Jiu, being extremely narrow and easily defensible was considered too difficult a proposition. The German plan, therefore, followed the usual lines of an envelopment of both flanks, its distinctive and unusual feature being the use of the cavalry. The initial difficulty which faced the Germans was to surmount the great mountain barrier which rises like a wall from the valley of the Rumanian Jiu. Once over the crest, the slopes down into Rumania would be comparatively easy. Paths led over the D. Arcanlului and D. Lescului, up to the head of the Vulcan Pass, and on the East of the Jiu valley from Livazeny to the head of the military road. Every effort was made to render these suitable for all arms, but in many places vehicles could only be got forward by using holdfasts and winding gear. The troops themselves were provided with special clothing to protect them against the rigours of the mountain climate.

The deployment for the attack is shown roughly on Map 7. The 6th Cavalry Division was preceded by an Austrian Infantry Battalion to clear a way through the mountains. The Cavalry was then to push forward into the plains and attack the Rumanians in the rear, taking no notice of the battle for the Szurduk Pass—a task somewhat similar to that which had been allotted to the Alpine Corps in the Battle of Sibiu. The weather had greatly improved and when the attack opened on the 23rd everything went according to plan.[1] By the evening of the 25th the leading Brigade of the Cavalry had emerged from the wooded hills and the Division could prepare for an attack on Borosteni and Francesti, which barred the way into the Bistrita valley, whilst in the centre the advance had got half way through the Szurduk Pass. On the evening of the 26th further progress had been made to the line Dobrita, Stanesti, Sambotin, Burnici, and the cavalry had taken Borosteni, though a Rumanian detachment from Orsova still held Francesti. Reinforcements had arrived in the shape of the 7th German Cavalry Division; the open country lay but a short distance in front, and though progress east of the Pass had been but slow, the sun was shining; the Kaiser had telegraphed congratulations; the Germans were, in short, thoroughly pleased with the situation. Falkenhayn's Cavalry Corps Commander, von Schmettow, was ordered up to take command of the two cavalry divisions. His instructions were not to wait for the opening of the Szurduk Pass, but, relying on the communications over the D. Arcanlului and the Vulcan Pass, to carry fire and sword into the plains of Wallachia and live on the country. The Rumanians, however, had not been idle, and on the next day (27th) the situation underwent a dramatic change. Whilst the original defenders of the pass had been falling back fighting, reinforcements had arrived from both Pitesti and from Orsova, raising the available forces to about 20 battalions. The advanced *échelon* of the Orsova detachment, arriving by forced marches, had already, as we have seen, held up the German Cavalry at Francesti. The remainder were disposed for an enveloping attack of the German right centre.

With the Pitesti detachment a general reserve had been formed near Targu Jiu, which now deployed so as to attack the German left in flank across the Jiu in a north westerly direction. When, therefore, the German columns spreading out on a 12-mile front confidently continued their advance in the morning mist in an endeavour to seize Targujiu and cut the pass road behind the detachment defending it at Bumbesti, they were assailed from both flanks, and the Rumanians also penetrated between the isolated columns, which fell back in confusion. In order to secure a good jumping off position for the expected reinforcing divisions an unsuccessful effort was made by the Germans to stand on the line Dobrita-Sambotin. Another line was then organised, from Hill 1191 to Plesa, the 7th Cavalry Division being ordered forward for the purpose; but on the 29th the Rumanians swept this away also.

The position of the 6th Cavalry Division was now precarious, and was rendered worse by a change in the weather, which turned to snow and rain. Unable to advance, its communications rendered useless by snow and mud, it commenced a painful retreat back into the mountains, abandoning guns and vehicles, and destroying horses to

---

[1] NOTE.—General Culcer on 24th October proposed a retirement to the Olt and was replaced in command of the 1st Army by General Dragalina, who was mortally wounded during the battle.

avoid their capture by the enemy. The Rumanian pursuit was, however, gravely affected by the weather conditions, which Falkenhayn admits saved the remnants of his forces, and on the 30th October, to his great relief, the line was stabilised as shown on the map. The Rumanians buried over 1,500 dead, and took 1,600 prisoners, with great quantities of war equipment of all kinds, the 11th Bavarian Division in particular suffering heavily as regards both men and material. Falkenhayn attributed the reverse very largely to the failure of his Orsova detachment to hold the Rumanians on their front. This, no doubt, was a contributory cause, as was also the bad timing of the Alpine Corps' attack, which had definitely failed before the Jiu offensive commenced. Strategically the Rumanians made good use of their local position on interior lines; tactically they were able to throw in a comparatively strong general reserve at the psychological moment when the enemy was fully stretched out in isolated columns unable to support each other, and on the wrong side of a formidable obstacle which might well convert defeat into disaster. On a smaller scale the Germans stood in much the same position as had been the Rumanian armies during their initial deployment and advance into Transylvania. Once the impetus of the advance was stopped by the defeat of any one important fraction, the whole edifice toppled and then crashed. Unfortunately for the Rumanians, the enemy, though defeated, had secured some important gains. He had advanced his jumping-off line some 10 miles through the Szurduk Pass. In his new positions on the forward slopes he was able to improve communication over the mountains behind him for a renewed attempt by the reinforcing divisions; he had acquired a knowledge of the country in front of him and of the preparations necessary before a fresh attack could be launched with good chance of success. These preparations were now put in hand with the greatest energy, with a view to attacking on 11th November.

Leaving the Jiu for the moment, let us see what was happening on other parts of the front, in order to bring the story up to the critical date, 11th November, when the supreme effort was to be made to burst into the plains and crush the Rumanian resistance before winter descended on the mountains. Space only permits of a very brief summary, but reference to Map 6 will, it is hoped, make the resulting situation tolerably clear.

Events in the Dobrudja from 10th October to 10th November.

The failure of the Rumanian combined offensive in the Dobrudja and across the Danube at Rohovo at the beginning of October has already been mentioned.

About the middle of October Mackensen received reinforcements and on the 19th attacked the Russo-Rumanian positions covering the important Constanza–Cernavoda railway. The salient features of the battle were that the Russian Commander was completely surprised, being in the act of moving the Cavalry Division and the 3rd Siberian Division across to the other bank of the Danube, to meet a supposed German attempt to cross. His numerical superiority was, therefore, partly nullified and the German artillery did the rest. A Russian division in the centre was routed, carrying with it the units on either flank; the 9th and 19th Rumanian Divisions were also driven back; and the Serbian Division, standing like a rock at Topraisar, was almost surrounded and annihilated.

The defeat was complete and led to the precipitate retirement of the whole line. On the 21st the enemy reached Medgidia; on the 23rd, Constanza, Rumania's most important seaport, was taken, and with it were lost important stores of grain and oil, which were either burnt or fell to the enemy. The 2nd and 5th Rumanian Divisions held Cernavoda as a bridgehead until the 25th, when it, too, was evacuated for fear of a second Turtukai. By the 26th the bulk of the Russo-Rumanian army was 20 miles north of the railway, and was only halted on the 29th after a retreat of 60 miles on the line Ostrov–Babadag, owing to the arrival of Russian reinforcements and the discontinuation of the pursuit.

The strategic results of this defeat were important. The intended Russo-Rumanian offensive into Transylvania, which might have relieved pressure on the rest of the Rumanian front, was delayed by the diversion of troops to the Dobrudja. The moral effect was equally great, and not the least unfortunate aspect was that fuel was lent to the fires of distrust between Rumanians and Russians, each blaming the other. At Rumania's request, Zaiontchkovsky, who was held to have neglected the most elementary military precautions, was replaced by Sakharof of Manchurian fame.

Of the four Rumanian divisions, all of which had suffered very heavily, one division was reconstituted out of the 9th and 19th (9/19), and the 2nd and 5th were withdrawn to form the 2/5th Division.

Meantime Mackensen, selecting the shortest line covering the Constanza–Cernavoda railway, left four divisions and a cavalry division to hold it, and with the remainder marched back to south of Bucharest in readiness to cross the Danube. When Sakharof advanced on the 7th November, the delaying forces fell back to the prepared position, devastating the country behind them, and so held him up until events in Rumania automatically stopped the Russian attacks.

Whether the Germans had ever intended to force the Danube behind Bucharest in continuation of the offensive of the 19th October is an open question. Hindenburg says that any idea of a further advance with a view to crossing the lower reaches of the Danube into Rumania was abandoned owing to the difficulty of getting bridging material forward, due to the command of the Danube by the Rumanian batteries and the absence of railways in North Dobrudja. It is probable that the delay in the advance of the other arm of the pincers on Bucharest was the determining factor, and that the more modest scheme of cutting off western Wallachia had to be adopted in consequence. In any case Mackensen's strategy had been brilliantly successful. His initial attack had wrecked the Rumanian offensive into Transylvania; his subsequent retirement had caused them to divert forces to the southern front, in the hopes of finishing him off—forces which might have saved the situation at the battles of Sibiu and Brasov. His second offensive delayed the Russo-Rumanian offensive in the North, and his second retirement kept strong forces occupied whilst the main decision was being obtained elsewhere. By noisily banging at the back door he effectually distracted the defenders at the front entrance at the most critical moments. It would be hard to find in history a better example of the effective use of detachments.

The Operations of the Fourth Rumanian Army.

The retirement of the Fourth Army was not seriously interfered with, the pursuing Austrians having no great zest for fighting, and the Rumanians occupied positions covering the Moldavian Passes at leisure, while in the north the 14th Division repulsed without difficulty any attempts to force the Tolgyes and Bekas Passes.

Farther south the Rumanian situation was more difficult. Hindenburg's plan had aimed at cutting in through the Oituz and Uz Passes behind the Ghimes Pass and so severing the main line of communication of the Fourth Army up the valley of the Trotus. It will be seen from the map that this important valley runs for a considerable distance within easy reach of the frontier, from which a number of practicable routes run down into it, the chief being the Uz and Oituz Passes. The Rumanians were fully alive to the danger and had concentrated the 7th and 15th Divisions, with the 8th Division and the 2nd Cavalry Division in reserve, in the area.

From the 12th to the 26th October they made a determined resistance to the Austrian efforts to advance, and held their positions intact. The enemy, indeed, at one time penetrated through the Uz Pass and reached the railway; but a well-executed counterattack late on 18th October drove them back, with the loss of 1,000 prisoners and 12 guns.

Persisting in their intention to force the Moldavian frontier, the enemy put in the 10th Bavarian Division, which formed the reserve of the First Austrian Army, without any result. The 8th Bavarian Division, Falkenhayn's only reserve, was, to his great annoyance, also removed on 21st October and sent up in all available motor transport to restore the situation in the Oituz Pass.

The Fourth Army had held its own well. Moreover, it was being progressively relieved from the right by the Russians, who were gradually forming their striking force. But the concentration of the latter was much delayed by poor staffwork, by break of gauge on the Ukranian frontier and by the miserable capacity of the Rumanian railways, which the Russians described as being even worse than their own. The diversion of troops to the Dobrudja also delayed matters. Still the position on the Moldavian front was satisfactory from the point of view of the defence, for if the Rumanian divisions had lost heavily, the Austrians were in no better case, and were quite incapable of further efforts.

The relieved Rumanian divisions were originally earmarked to show the Russians the way over into the Maros Valley, but, as will be seen from the map, they quickly found urgent employment elsewhere at the Predeal Pass and in the Valley of the Olt.

The Second Army Front.

Passing southwards, there had been considerable fighting at the Bodza, Bratocea and Predelus Passes, which had kept the tired 6th and 3rd Rumanian Divisions fully employed. In the Predeal Pass there had been heavy engagements from the 10th October onwards, in which the enemy forced the Rumanian 10th and 21st Divisions back to Busteni These divisions were about to be relieved by the 10th and 4th Divisions, and we shall meet them again playing a prominent part at the Battle of the Arges; for the moment they were exhausted. In front of Campulung the 12th and 22nd Divisions were holding their own and preventing any further enemy advance by successful, if costly, counterattacks. As the result of the latter, Falkenhayn was asked for reinforcements, which he refused.

First Army.

On the Olt front the Alpine Corps, after its first unsuccessful effort, had again resumed the offensive, which resulted in considerable gains. A costly and unsuccessful counterattack by the Rumanians on the 28th was followed up by the Germans and the whole Rumanian right centre fell back, leaving a considerable number of prisoners in the enemy's hands. On the 29th the latter captured Titesti, whilst, farther south, on 6th November, a turning movement from the east resulted in the rounding up of 1,000 prisoners and the annihilation of several Rumanian detachments. On 10th November the Germans put in the newly arrived 216th Division with a view to exploiting their success. To meet the situation the 14th Rumanian Division from the Fourth Army had been brought up, whilst the 8th Division, arriving shortly after, started to prepare a rear position near Tigveni. The 13th and 23rd Divisions were made up to some sort of strength from the 20th Division, which now disappeared.

The Jiu front, where the Germans were preparing their main offensive, was held by mixed detachments of the 1st and 11th Divisions. The only preparations made to meet the coming onslaught, which, in the absence of air observation, was apparently quite unsuspected, were a project for forming a general reserve at Pitesti.

Looking at the general picture shown on Map 6, the comparative absence of a general reserve on either side is remarkable.

Falkenhayn's consisted of the 3rd German Cavalry Division (three regiments) at Brasov, but a succession of divisions were moving from other fronts which completely safeguarded him, even had the Rumanians been in a position to attack. The watchfulness of G.H.Q. as to the security of the First Austrian Army, in view of the growing Russian concentration, is understandable; but here, again, it would be an easy matter to divert reinforcing divisions as they arrived.

The Rumanian situation was obviously much more serious, their sole reserve consisting of the 8th, 10th, and 21st Divisions, which were being relieved and urgently in need of a rest; the 17th Division at Pitesti, the 2/5th reforming in the Dobrudja and the two cavalry divisions—a very meagre reserve for a front of nearly 300 miles, excluding the Danube front. The chronic absence of any reserve was, perhaps, the most striking feature of Rumanian strategy, any reserve formed by the armies being promptly seized upon and thrown by G.H.Q. into the furnace on some other part of the front. It would seem that the Russians would have been well advised to repair this obvious deficiency by some more direct means than their Transylvanian offensive, of which more anon. Their answer still doubtless was—" shorten the front." It must further be noted that the number of Rumanian divisions gives very little indication of their fighting value. Most of them had been continuously in action without relief for long periods, during which their losses had always been heavy owing to having to compensate for lack of fire-power by weight of numbers. Judging from the reports of foreign observers, the normal course of events appears to have been for the Germans to open a surprise attack covered by a concentration of artillery, under which the Rumanians, who had practically no telephones and whose ideas of entrenching seem to have been rudimentary, evacuated their positions. Reinforcements were then hurried up, usually in excessive numbers, and counterattacks were launched. Whilst these often succeeded, the Rumanians suffered inordinate losses from machine-gun and artillery fire, and the survivors were worn out by marching and countermarching. All ranks were becoming imbued with the belief that it was impossible to stand against the enemy's heavy artillery. Lest this remark should appear unnecessarily severe, it may be mentioned, on the authority of Hindenburg, that the Bulgarians showed a similar weakness in face of the Allied artillery on the Salonika front. That the Rumanian soldier allowed himself to be sent forward time after time on such enterprises speaks volumes for his individual courage. Losses had already amounted to some 200,000, and though trained men to replace them existed, the extent to which they could be used depended on the available rifles, which were insufficient. Consequently, whilst battalions in the Northern Army averaged 1,000, those in the First and Second Armies were no stronger than 700.

The composition of divisions varied from 12 to 25 battalions, and averaged about 13. In artillery they equally lacked homogeneity, the divisional artillery varying from 6 to 12 batteries. All this, of course, greatly complicated staffwork. It was not a case of *a* division but of *which* division. In some cases it had been found necessary to double up formations (9/19, 2/5), the 20th had disappeared, and in the 4th—ominous sign !—cholera had made its appearance.

Efforts were being made to reorganise the army on a more logical basis and to form reserves, but, whilst heavy fighting was going on everywhere, the difficulties were enormous. The Rumanian Army badly required a winter in which to reorganise and refit : it failed to get it by just about a fortnight.

If the situation of the army was not encouraging, the *morale* of the population was certainly no better. As early as the 14th October orders had been issued for the evacuation of the Government to Jassi, and, though countermanded on the receipt of more encouraging information, everyone was on tenterhooks, whilst the poorer-spirited politicians openly discussed the necessity for a separate peace.

The arrival of the Russians dragged on interminably amidst mutual recriminations, the Russian staff attributing the delay to the fact that their reinforcements had to march from the frontier owing to the different gauge of the Ukranian railways which involved transhipment at the frontier, and also to inability of the Rumanians to supply rolling stock. Indeed the Rumanian railways were totally unable to cope with the masses of troops which were now converging on the country, or being hurried from side to side. The date for the grand counter-offensive was postponed from the 31st October to some later date which no one could specify; meanwhile the Russian troops were eating up the country.

So far as may be judged from telegrams sent at this time, the Russians displayed no particular anxiety as to the situation. Indeed the opinion expressed at Russian Headquarters was that the German plan had failed owing, firstly, to Falkenhayn's inability to break through towards Bucharest and, secondly, to the failure of Mackensen to annihilate the forces opposed to him in the Dobrudja. In these circumstances it was thought that the initiative could be regained by Russian offensives into North Transylvania and in the Dobrudja, which would automatically relieve pressure on the Rumanian front and so enable them to tide over the period before winter came to their assistance. The Ninth Russian Army in the North, under General Letchitsky, was to consist of at least 11 infantry and 5 cavalry divisions, and any available Rumanian divisions were to co-operate. The date suggested for the attack—the Russians were very vague—was the 14th November, and Brussilof's other armies further North were to advance simultaneously. The divergent offensives may be open to criticism. It is not at all clear what the Dobrudja attack as a main operation was expected to effect, except to play the German game. One suspects an ulterior motive, and the promise of Constantinople, to which the Dobrudja was the shortest route, may supply the answer to the problem.

As regards the Northern offensive, Falkenhayn, for one, considered that it had no chance of producing any effect in time to forestall his own attack. The season was too far advanced, and the Rumanians would have to cross 100 miles of mountainous country of no strategic value, before reaching the important Maros valley. Moreover, he points out that the destruction of the railway viaducts west of the Ghimes Pass rendered the supply and maintenance of large forces impossible. Consequently, despite the parlous condition of the Austrians holding the

Northern front, he thought that his superiors were overcautious in retaining the 8th and 10th Bavarian Divisions in the North. The feasibility of a large scale Russian offensive was never actually put to the test, so we must leave it at that. Assuming, however, that the Russians had succeeded in initiating a powerful attack in the North at the same time as Sakharof advanced in the Dobrudja and, assuming that the Rumanian centre held its grounds long enough to enable these offensives to develop fully, the initiative might perhaps have been secured, and with it the salvation of Rumania.

Unfortunately the Russian plan was based on wrong information as regards the enemy, which was perhaps excusable; and equally faulty ideas—or indifference—as regards the resisting powers of the Rumanians, which was criminal.

The German Plans.

The German plans have been so fully dealt with in the course of the foregoing narrative that little remains to be said. The cessation of attacks on the Salonika and Italian fronts due to the approach of winter; the exhaustion of the Russians, combined with their lack of ammunition and the state of the roads, which had not yet frozen; the obvious improbability of the Franco-British offensive on the Somme achieving any great result at so late a period in the year, all combined to set free German troops. In Rumania alone could a clear cut decision be obtained, and then only if the Transylvanian barrier were to be crossed before the end of November. The conclusion was obvious, and the Germans lost no time in acting upon it. Thanks to the excellent railway system in Transylvania, reinforcing divisions could be detrained with precision as regards time and place, and they were successively brought up (*vide* map 6) in an ever-increasing stream. The 8th, 10th, 11th and 12th Bavarian Divisions, the 41st and 109th German Divisions, and 6th and 7th Cavalry Divisions and other smaller formations and units were to be followed by the 115th and 216th Divisions, and various Austrian Divisions. The nature of the plan, which consisted of a general attack all along the front with the main blow down the Jiu, is clearly shown by the movements of the reinforcing divisions (map 6). South of the Danube stood Mackensen with 1 German, 2 Bulgarian, 1 Turkish Division, and 1 mixed Cavalry Division ready to advance on Bucharest, in conjunction with Falkenhayn, as soon as the latter was far enough forward to hold out a hand. Thus the Germans hoped to repeat the converging movement so brilliantly successful at Sadowa in 1866 and in the winter battles of 1914 amongst the Masurian lakes.

The Second Battle of Targujiu, 10th–17th November. (Map 8.)

We left Fakenhayn making preparations for an attack down the Jiu Valley with fresh troops. His reasons for selecting this particular front were briefly as follows. The main mountain barrier was narrower here than elsewhere, and it was possible for troops to get through in one long march. Then, again, the country on either side was known, and the Germans held the exit of the pass; lastly, it was probable that the Rumanians would not expect a second attack from this direction after the disastrous failure of the first. Whilst the new commander of the Petroseni group, General Kuhne, was making his preparations, Falkenhayn was engaged in the usual wrangle with superior authority, which we need not go into, the fact being only mentioned to show that the German machine by no means always worked smoothly.

Since all efforts to obtain a surprise by dispersion had failed, this new attempt was to follow the accepted principle of concentration and rely chiefly on weight, though it was hoped that the element of surprise would not be entirely lacking. The previous failure had shown the danger of depending on mountain tracks, and the experiences of the cavalry in particular did not encourage their further employment for turning movements in mountain warfare.

The problem was thus to get the bulk of four infantry divisions followed by two cavalry divisions—60,000 men and 30,000 horses—with all their vehicles, through a defile 20 miles long, along a single road which allowed only one stream of traffic in each direction, and get them through quickly before the Rumanians could bring up reinforcements. Throughout the 20 miles the valley opened out at only one small spot, two-thirds of the way through; otherwise there were no places for bivouacking or for parking vehicles or stores off the road. This, it will be agreed, presented a very serious staff problem, even though the Germans held the southern exit. The arrangements for it took the best part of a fortnight, which was spent in getting the artillery forward into position, improving the road, forming dumps, and making arrangements for traffic control.

This latter was worked out in the greatest detail on the lines of a railway timetable, the necessary day and night signals, telephone connections, etc., being duly installed. The general scheme of attack was for the two leading divisions, the 41st and 109th, to advance and deploy on either side of the road, supported by a powerful concentration of artillery, whilst the 11th Bavarian and the 301st were to follow, in column of route, and fan out as soon as the leading divisions had cleared the enemy from their positions commanding the end of the Pass. The Cavalry Corps was to wait north of the Pass until the infantry had gained sufficient room for them to get through and manœuvre. A fifth infantry division (115th) was being railed up behind as a reserve.

The Rumanian forces available to oppose this human avalanche consisted of the equivalent of one tired division. In addition, there were available as potential reinforcements three battalions from the Cerna; one battalion from the Olt, where the Rumanians were fully employed in stopping the Alpine Corps; and the 17th Division at Pitesti.

The attack opened on the 10th November by the capture of the Muncelul and Urina Boului, and on the following day the great movement began. By the evening of the 11th the two leading divisions (41st and

109th) had secured the line D. Lesului–Bumbesti–Postaia, thence running N.E. on a front of 15 miles. The Rumanians were fighting well, particularly east of the pass, where they were still in position to bring long-range fire to bear on its exits. The permanent fortifications at Bumbesti had been effectively demolished by the concentrated fire of the German artillery, and the two supporting divisions, waiting west of the pass, were ordered to advance. All next day and the following night an unbroken stream of troops and transport, favoured by perfect weather and a full moon, poured through the pass, the 301st Division then moving to the east, the 11th Bavarian Division to the south-west. Meanwhile the two leading divisions continued to gain ground slowly in the face of obstinate opposition, which was crushed by the German artillery. By the evening of the 13th the front ran east and west through Sambotin, whilst the 11th Bavarian Division was concentrated north-west of Sambotin and the 301st Division was near Dragoesti, facing east. The next day (14th) the line had advanced to Turcinesti, the Rumanian resistance was weakening; whereupon orders were sent back to the Cavalry Corps assembled north of the pass to advance as rapidly as possible, its instructions being as follows :—

"The Cavalry Corps will take up an energetic pursuit.

"Our first objective is Filiasu. The task of the Cavalry Corps is to harass the retreat of the enemy, who is falling back in front of the LIVth Corps (41st, 109th, 11th Bavarian, 301st Division).

"The Cavalry Corps must so direct its march as to be able to envelop the enemy if he makes a stand against the LIVth Corps."

In pursuance of these orders the Cavalry Corps passed through the front, and 24 hours later (night 15th/16th) its 7th Division was deployed south and south-west of Targujiu, with the 6th Cavalry Division on its left, whilst a detachment sent out to cut the railway successfully accomplished its mission at a point between Targujiu and Petrestii. Comparing this movement with the periodic advances of our own Cavalry Corps in France, and remembering that it had to be carried out by a single road, it will be agreed that it represented no inconsiderable achievement.

The most difficult part of the operation appeared to be over. Air reconnaissances reported the Rumanians to be falling back everywhere, and the break through at last appeared to be complete. Next morning (16th), however, when the German cavalry attempted to push on southwards, they found that this was by no means the case, for in actual fact the Rumanians were endeavouring to repeat the successful enveloping manœuvre of the first battle of Targujiu. With this object the Rumanian 11th Division was ordered to hold the hills between the Gilort and the Motrul Valleys on the line Seasa–Vacarea–Valeni–Carbesti, whilst the Cerna detachment held Cetatea, and the 17th Division attacked from the Gilort Valley, where it was beginning to arrive, its progress having been delayed by a railway accident half-way between Pitesti and Slatina. Meanwhile the Olt detachment was directed to hold up the advance of the 301st Division eastwards.

The German commander, finding the way barred by the Rumanian position in the hills, immediately gave orders to the cavalry to attack, with the object of enveloping the Rumanian left, but the cavalry failed to capture the hills near Cetatea and Carbesti and met with no success in the centre.

The 41st, 109th and 11th Bavarian Divisions were then ordered forward to relieve the 6th Cavalry Division, and to attack the Rumanian centre frontally, but rain and snow delayed the movement and only the 11th Bavarian Division on the left got into action towards Petrestii against the leading *échelons* of the 17th Rumanian Division, which was hurried forward unit by unit as it detrained. The 301st Division and a cavalry detachment made no progress, and hours which might be vital were being lost.

In these circumstances the Germans decided to pull out the cavalry and try a wider sweep westwards round the Rumanian left. The 6th Cavalry Division was successfully relieved, although in actual touch with the enemy, the operation being covered by the snowstorms, and marched back to Targujiu. Thence it made a *détour* behind the 7th Cavalry Division, and next morning was ready to advance from Vladoi, having covered a distance of 20 miles in bad weather along vile roads. Rumanian reinforcements were arriving, and it was only a question of time for their pressure against the German left from the Gilort valley to become a serious menace. The promptness with which the cavalry manœuvre was decided upon and carried out had a determining effect on the operations, thus showing the transcendant importance of mobility when combined with firm and quick decision.

It snowed heavily on the night 16th/17th and all rearward signal communications were interrupted, but next morning (17th), a frontal attack by the German 41st and 109th Divisions in the direction of Trocani had by 11 a.m. driven a wedge through the Rumanian centre. At the same time the cavalry and armoured cars from Vladoi advanced 25 miles *viâ* Brosteni down the Motrul valley, thus completely turning the Rumanian left, whilst a detachment sent back north-east from Rosiuta attacked the Cetatea positions in the rear, and thus cleared the way for the 7th Cavalry Division. The Rumanians holding the hills about Valeni were surrounded, and the whole left and centre broke up, 3,500 prisoners and several guns being captured by the Germans. Now threatened from the north-west and west, the 17th Rumanian Division, with the survivors of the 11th Division, fell back across the Gilort to the east and south-east, blowing up the bridges.

On the 19th Filiasu was occupied by the Germans, and Craiova on the 21st November.

The defence put up by the Rumanians, however, had gained sufficient time to permit of the evacuation of all warlike stores, and the blowing up of many of the bridges. Whether the First Army with the resources at its disposal could have stopped the enemy may remain an open question. Luck was with the latter in the matter of the weather, for had the snow come a few days earlier the difficulties of passing through and deploying from the Szurduk Pass would have been greatly increased. The Rumanians started badly owing to the failure of their Intelligence to give them any warning of the impending attack, and the attention of the First Army Command appears to have been engrossed until too late by the situation in the Olt Valley. Thus the 17th Division did not commence to arrive in the Gilort until the 16th, six days after the German attack started; partly no doubt owing to the railway accident, it was put in by driblets, and therefore never had the effect which a concentrated attack might have produced. The attention of Rumanian G.H.Q. also was taken up until too late by events nearer Bucharest, where failure would be much more disastrous, and the First Army received no assistance from this direction, though G.H.Q. might perhaps argue that the First Army already had its full share of the scanty reserves. Falkenhayn's repeated tapping along the front had achieved his object of exhausting the Rumanian soldiery, of keeping their staff guessing, and of making them eventually guess wrong. On the other hand, the Rumanian resistance had forced him to make his effort a long way from Mackensen and Bucharest, *i.e.*, in strategically the least favourable position, whilst the arrival of the 17th Rumanian Division had tactically prevented any envelopment of the Jiu group on its inner flank.

Even so, the situation from the Rumanian point of view was sufficiently serious. The western end of Wallachia was cut off, and the road to Bucharest lay open across the plains, with only one good defensive position, the Olt, on which to stop the enemy. Moreover, the 115th German Division had detrained at Petroseni and was already moving forward on the 18th. Every day the avalanche was gathering strength; and, unless it could be stopped, must seriously affect the situation in the passes on either side.

The position of that portion of the 1st Rumanian Division posted at Orsova was obviously hopeless. Its subsequent operations form one of the brightest episodes of the war on the Rumanian side, but can only be briefly sketched. The detachment continued to block the Danube until 22nd November, and then commenced its retirement in front of the Austro-German force which it had for so long successfully opposed, being threatened in the rear by a mixed German detachment of one regiment cavalry, one battalion infantry, and a few guns, detached from Targujiu to cut it off. It turned the tables on the latter by driving the infantry battalion into Turnu Severin, where it only maintained itself with the assistance of the Bulgarians. The Rumanians then fought their way back as far as the lower Olt, where on 6th December they found the way barred by a chance detachment from Mackensen's Army which had meantime crossed the Danube. There they were forced to capitulate on the day after Bucharest fell, 10,000 men and 40 guns falling into the enemy's hands. They had remained a force in being until the last possible moment when they could exercise any influence on the operations of their main army.

To the east the retreat of the First Army from the Jiu uncovered the left and rear of the Rumanians astride the Olt exit from the mountains, where they were successfully holding up the Alpine Corps and the newly arrived 216th Division. This latter had been put in here by Falkenhayn owing to the fact that the railways could not deal with any more troops on the Petroseni-Jiu front. The Germans again assumed the offensive on the 15th November and, despite the employment of the 8th Division, pressed the Rumanians back, the latter gradually evacuating the hills west of the Olt and swinging back their left so as to be in a position to join hands with the remainder of the First Army should it succeed in making a stand on the river line against the enemy advancing from Craiova.

Further east, again, the Germans, with the aid of the fresh 12th Bavarian Division, made strenuous efforts to reach Pitesti from the direction of Campulung, but were brought to a full stop by 17th November; so much so that there was some talk of taking the 12th Bavarian Division back, and sending it round *viâ* Petroseni through the Szurduk Pass towards Craiova. Falkenhayn, however, vetoed this move, as it might take the best part of a fortnight, and ordered pressure to be maintained here to prevent the Rumanians from withdrawing troops for the defence of the Olt. Thus on this front also there was nothing yet in the shape of a *débâcle*.

In the Brasov Group of passes snow had practically put a stop to active operations, and Falkenhayn withdrew the 187th Division into Army reserve. Further north, the Russians had commenced local preliminary offensives which led to bitter fighting, but had no effect on the general situation, beyond keeping the Austrians and the 8th and 10th Bavarian Divisions fully occupied. The main offensive, for which 15 Divisions and 5 Cavalry Divisions were at last in position, was again delayed—possibly intentionally—by the summoning of Brussilof and Letchitsky to Russian G.H.Q. for a conference. It was eventually fixed for the 28th November, but before that date it had been progressively weakened by withdrawals to relieve the Rumanian Army.

As soon as the extent of the danger in the Jiu Valley became apparent to the Rumanian G.H.Q., which was not until 18th November, it was decided to concentrate all available reserves at Pitesti and launch a counterattack. By the 20th, however, it became evident that it was too late to save the situation in the Jiu, and the alternative plan was adopted of standing on the only good defensive line—that of the River Olt—to cover the regrouping of the Rumanian armies and organise a striking force. This measure would further gain time for the Russians to relieve the 9/19th Division in the Dobrudja, to take over down to the Predelus Pass, and to permit of the launching of their long-deferred offensive in the north. With this object a front was hastily formed under the orders of General Presan, the successful commander of the Fourth Army, as shown generally on Map 9.

The total forces available for the Olt front from Curtea d'Arges to the Danube amounted nominally to some 120 battalions, 55 squadrons, and 108 batteries—the equivalent, say, of eight infantry and two cavalry divisions, all very tired and disorganised—to hold a front of 100 miles, which they had no time to strengthen or occupy systematically. Advancing from the west and north were Falkenhayn's six German and two Austrian infantry divisions and two cavalry divisions. Taking into consideration the overwhelming superiority of the enemy in all technical and material equipment, and their *morale* raised by victory, the Rumanian chances of success were not great.

The view expressed at Russian G.H.Q. was as follows:

"The Rumanians are now being forced back to positions which they should long ago have occupied and fortified. This line is well adapted to defence, and, in spite of training, equipment, etc., the Rumanians may be able to stand there till the Russians are ready to move and relieve pressure."

This view, however, entirely neglected to take into account Mackensen's Danube army.

The German Advance through Western Wallachia and the Crossing of the Olt (November 21st–26th).

We will now return to Falkenhayn's army (Kuhne's group), which we left entering Craiova. It was advancing south and south-east, spread out on a broad front, and much hampered by bad weather as well as by the demolitions effected by the Rumanians in their retreat. The cavalry had been equally delayed and Falkenhayn remarks that previous experiences had been confirmed—viz., that over a series of days cavalry in the mass can move no quicker than infantry. His air reconnaissances had told him of the movement of Rumanian reinforcements towards Pitesti and the Olt, whilst their preparations to swing back their line from the exits of the Red Tower Pass were also reported.

G.H.Q. now informed him that Mackensen was about to cross the Danube, and gave as a dividing line between the two armies the projected railway line Craiova–Caracal–Rosi de Vede–Bucharest. Kuhne's group was to attack in the direction Ploesti–Bucharest, the Alpine Corps co-operating with a view to clearing the remaining passes through the Transylvanian Alps. Falkenhayn disagreed with this strategic conception, pointing out that it would mean crossing a series of transverse spurs and valleys along semi-mountain roads, whereas an advance in the plains closer to the Danube would be just as effective in clearing the passes, and be far easier and quicker. He saw no reason to alter the orders issued on the 21st, which were to the following effect:—

The Cavalry Corps to advance and capture the bridges at Caracal and Slatina on the 23rd, reconnoitring up to the Danube on the right, and cutting the Pitesti–Rosi de Vede railway as soon as possible.

The leading infantry of the Kuhne group to cross the line Slatina–Dragasani on the 24th.

Dellmensingen's group (Alpine Corps, etc.), after reaching the line Raminicu Valcea–Curtea d'Arges to advance towards Pitesti.

Farther east the Kronstadt (Brasov) passes were to be attacked.

The new 115th Division to move to Craiova in pursuance of the plan for reinforcing the manœuvring wing—viz., the right.

On the 23rd the bridge at Stoenesti was captured almost intact by the cavalry, and a small bridgehead formed, which was well held against a weak Rumanian counterattack. Why this bridge had not been either blown up or properly guarded is not known to the writer, but its loss was naturally fatal to any Rumanian plan for holding the comparatively strong line of the Olt. Mackensen, apprised of this success, immediately commenced to cross the Danube farther east. On the 25th and 26th the whole of Von Schmettow's cavalry divisions were east of the Olt and driving back the Rumanian cavalry. Touch had also been established with Mackensen.

Meantime Kuhne's main infantry mass, consisting of the 41st and 109th and 11th Bavarian Divisions, was compelled to march on one road most of the way from Craiova to Slatina, owing to the demolitions carried out by the Rumanian rearguards, who appear to have executed their task very thoroughly. The 109th Division was then diverted southwards to follow the cavalry towards Caracal, whilst on the left the 301st reached Dragasani, where it found the bridge effectively breached.

Attempts by the centre column (41st and 11th Bavarian Divisions) to effect a crossing at Slatina on the 24th and 25th failed, for the bridges had been broken and the German bridging train had not come up, the river was in flood, whilst from the high ground on the eastern bank the Rumanians swept the approaches. Eventually the 11th Bavarian Division was sent south to follow the 109th Division across at Stoenesti, to which point the 115th, following behind, was also directed.

On the 26th the Rumanians withdrew under the threat to their left flank, and on the same day Kuhne's group obtained touch by motor for the first time with von Dellmensingen's group on the Olt. The whole front from the Danube to the Transylvanian Alps was in touch—weak touch, it is true, but still in touch.

Falkenhayn all this time was receiving messages from G.H.Q. at Pless urging the importance of pressing forward to help Mackensen, asking why he did not obey orders, and endeavouring to direct the movements of individual divisions. Apparently G.H.Q. had visions of rounding up the whole Rumanian Army against the Transylvanian Alps by swinging Falkenhayn's right forward and advancing it in the direction of Ploesti with Mackensen on its right. On the night of the 26th/27th Ludendorf, short-circuiting the army group commander, the Archduke Charles, telephoned personally that the Kaiser wished the Cavalry Corps to push forward at once north of Bucharest without taking any notice of small intervening bodies of the enemy. All of which Falkenhayn considered showed that G.H.Q. knew nothing about the situation, either of his army or of the enemy. In his opinion the behaviour of the Rumanians seemed to show that no longer were they retreating in disconnected or uncontrolled columns, but were now being drawn back in pursuance of a definite plan. He was right, but perhaps he was only wise after the event.

Before concluding with these incidents, that led up to the battle of the Argesh, a few comments may not be out of place. As regards strategy, we have seen how the original German plan for pinching Rumania across the waist between the northern Dobrudja and the Brasov Passes had been abandoned in face of the Rumanian resistance in the latter area. The more modest, but still comprehensive, plan of cutting off the greater part of Wallachia in the region of Bucharest had similarly been defeated by the failure of the attacks down the Olt and Jiu in the latter part of October. The policy of dispersion had been no more successful in the case of the German efforts to advance than in that of the Rumanians. They only succeeded when they concentrated at one point whilst the defence was still dispersed. The actual break through had only been effected at the eleventh hour at the place least damaging to Rumania. Moreover, the tenacious resistance made by the defence in the Jiu Valley had enabled the Rumanians to extricate the forces in western Wallachia, with the single exception of the Orsova detachment.

It seems clear that the Rumanians should have taken steps to organise the defences of the Olt line before they were actually driven back on to it. Whether or no they would have been wiser to have retired earlier and in their own time to that line must remain a matter of opinion. The Russians certainly thought so, and their view was shared by the British General Staff and by at least one distinguished Rumanian commander. There is, however, much to be said on the other side, and we have an almost parallel case, when, after the German break through on the Western front in the spring of 1918, the advisability of retiring from the northern portion of the dangerous coastal zone behind a great series of inundations was actually considered, only to be immediately vetoed by Marshal Foch.

Retirements from highly organised positions to positions not so well organised are apt to be dangerous even with troops of good *morale*, and if, like Marshal Haig, the Rumanian C.-in-C. decided that it was better to issue a " backs to the wall " order, we should not lightly condemn it, nor conclude that any other course would have produced a better result without more intimate knowledge of the condition of the Rumanian Army at the time. The course of the subsequent battles in the plains tends rather to support the wisdom of the decision taken, as being possibly the lesser of two evils.

As regards tactics, in making plans for their successful offensive down the Jiu the Germans took facts as they existed, and events justified their conclusions Without in any way wishing to belittle their achievements, it is, however, permissible to consider what would have been the result had the Rumanians disposed of an adequate number of machine guns and aeroplanes. Would the leading divisions have succeeded in forcing their way out of the defiles against the fire of automatic weapons? If they had done so, what would have been the effect of air attack on the endless column of troops and transport marching in the moonlight along the narrow road through the Szurduk Pass, a cliff on one side and a precipice on the other? Or, again, on the cavalry masses waiting at the north of the pass? Overwhelming air superiority alone rendered the movement possible; air inferiority in the air, as in all other technical equipment, contributed largely to the Rumanian defeat.

The fact that in spite of such inferiority he held the passes for six long weeks, waiting for the Russian counteroffensive which came too late, must be placed to the credit of the Rumanian soldier.

(To be concluded.)

GENERAL MAP OF RUMANIA

Map 6

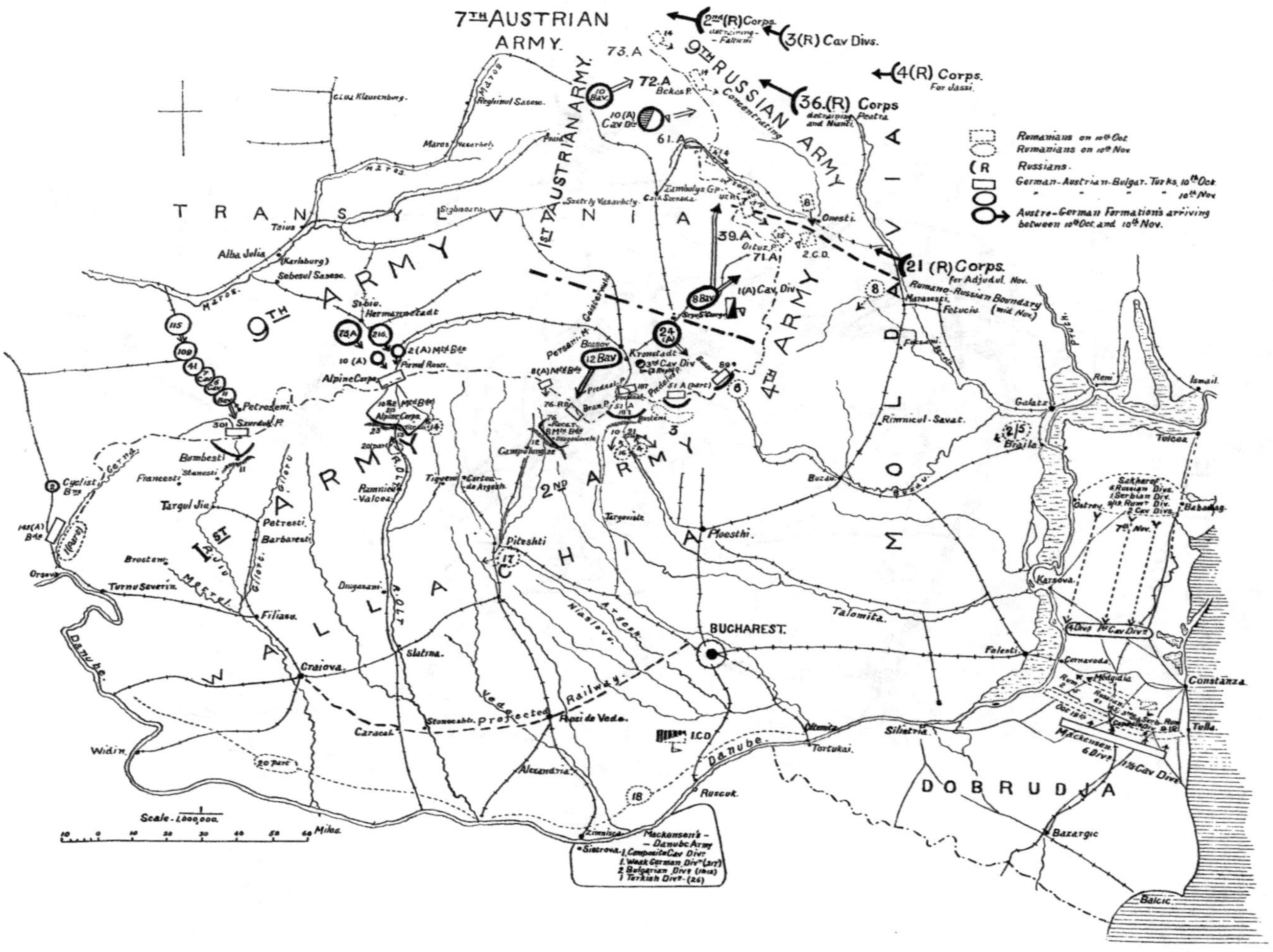

Map 7

FIRST BATTLE OF TARGU JIU
(OCTOBER 23rd – 30th)

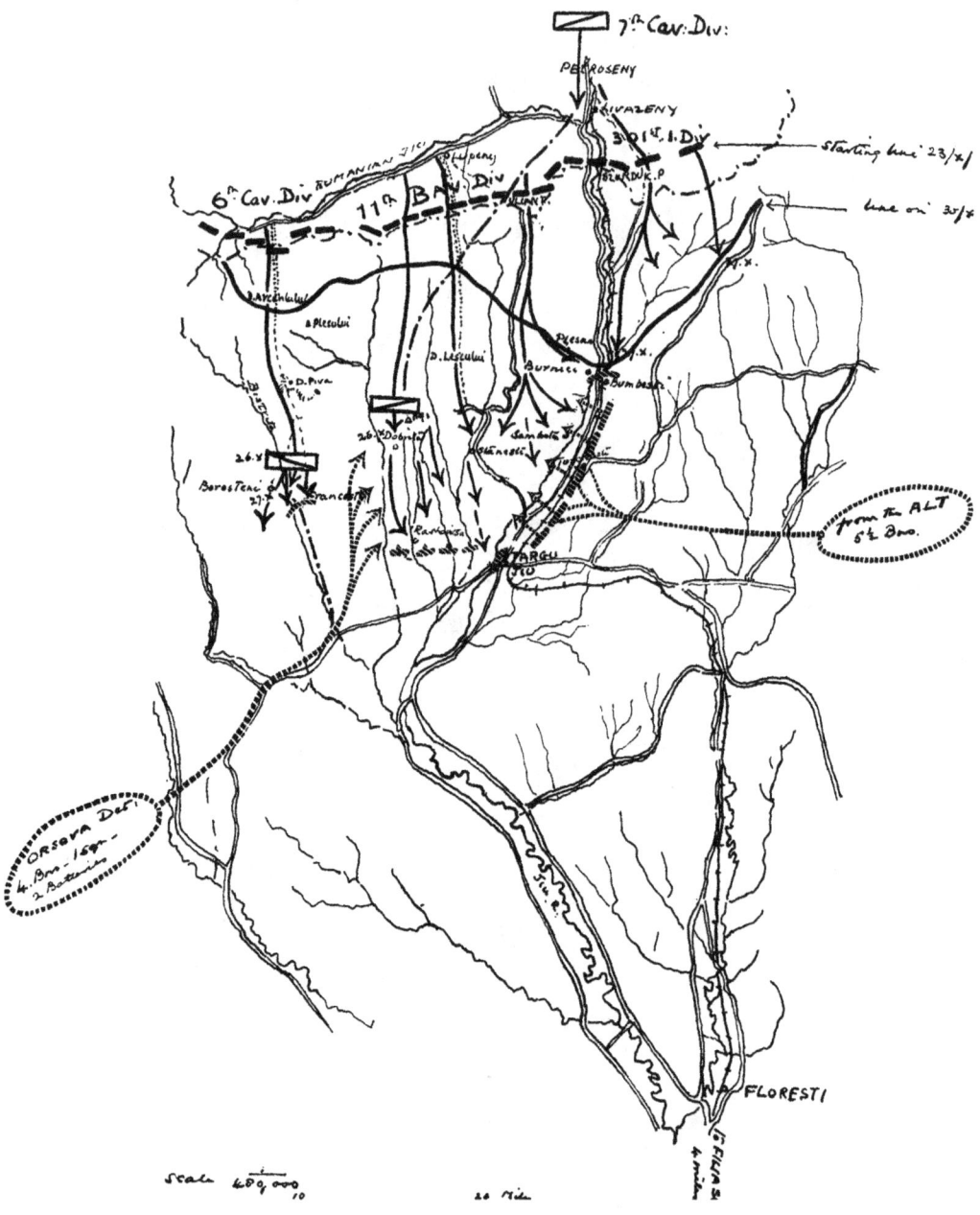

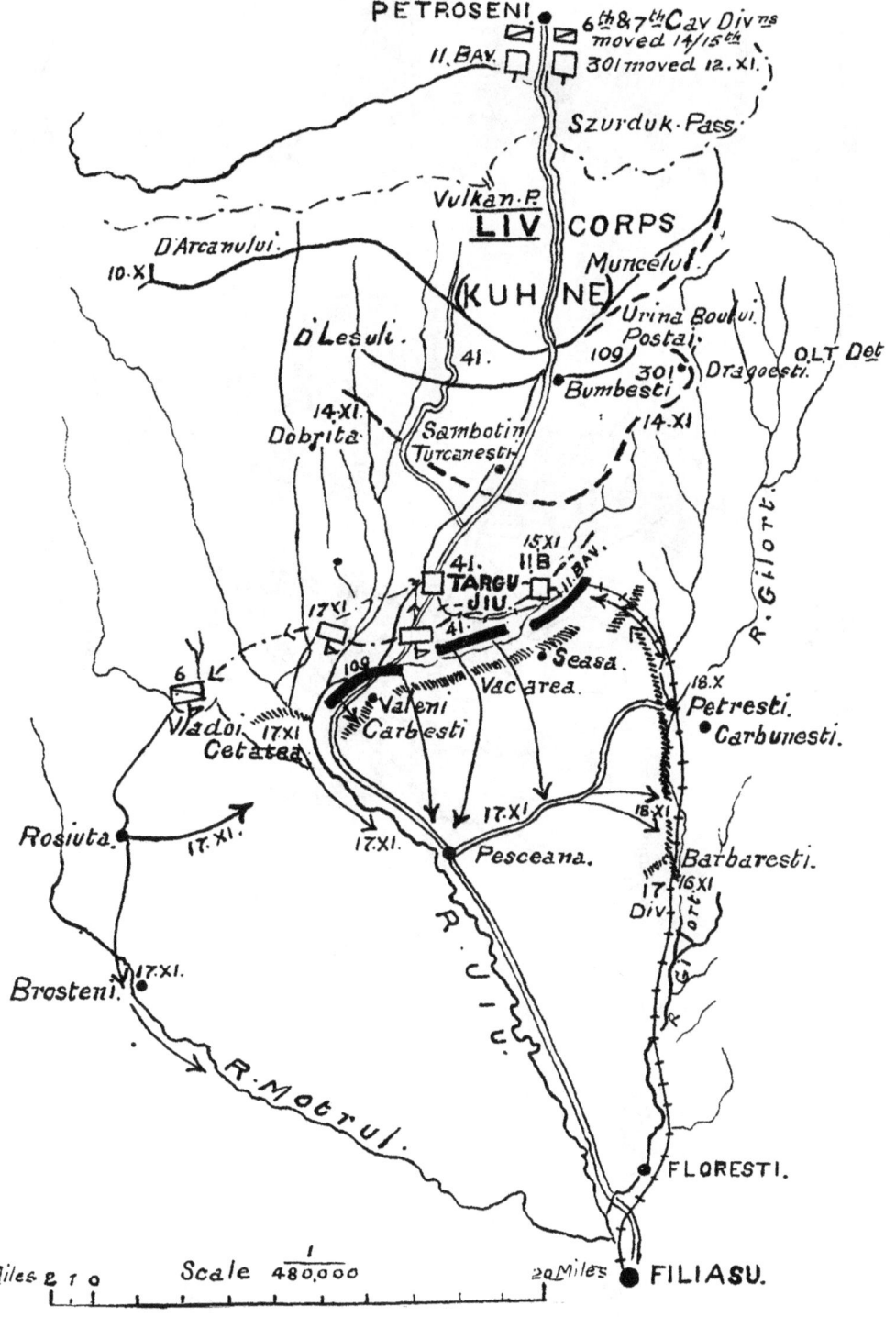

Map 9

THE ADVANCE OF KUHNE'S GROUP AFTER TARGU JIU
AND SITUATION ON NOVEMBER 24th ON THE OLT RIVER

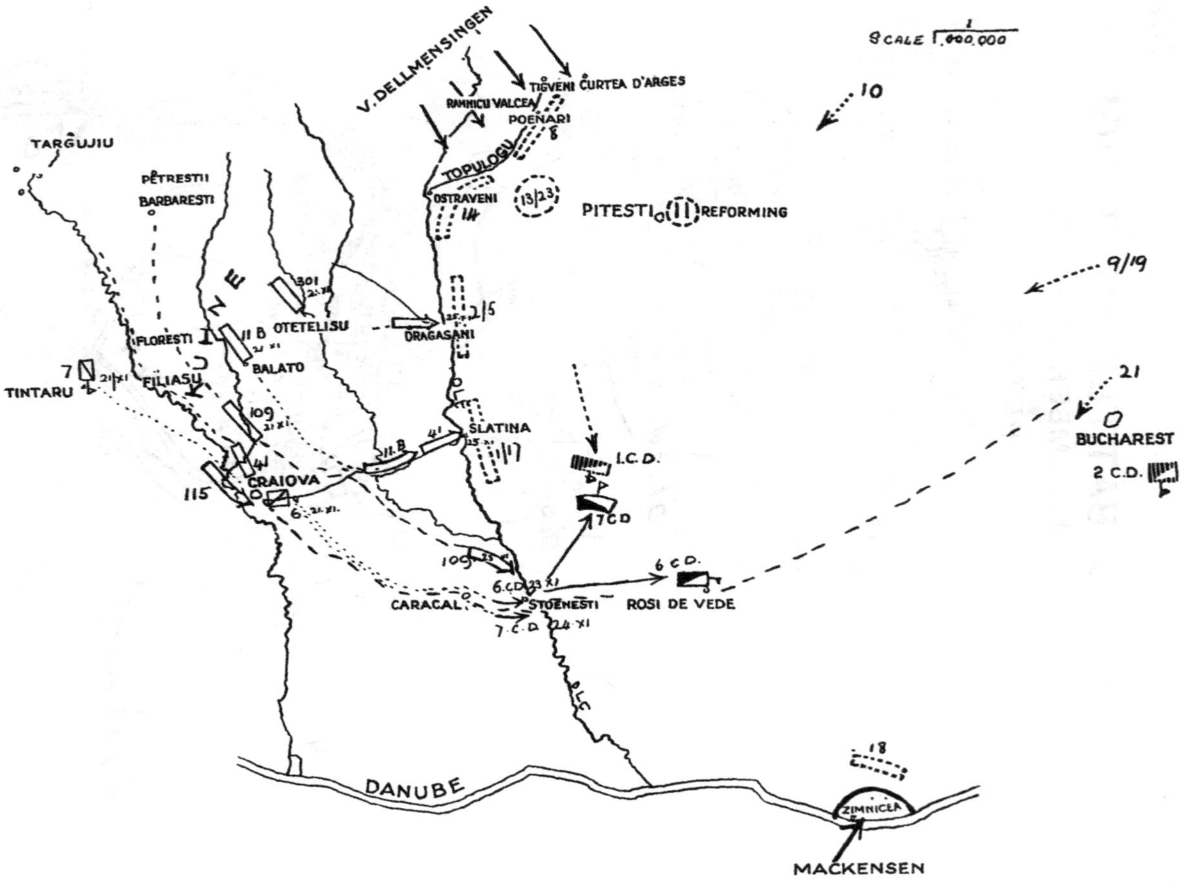

AN OUTLINE OF THE RUMANIAN CAMPAIGN, 1916–1918.

By Major-General W. M. St. G Kirke, C.B., C.M.G., D.S.O., p.s.c.

PART III

The Battles for the Defence of Bucharest and the Retreat to the Sereth.

Events up to the 26th November. (Map 10.)

The Rumanian High Command, in consultation with General Berthelot,[1] had decided to use the General Reserve when concentrated near Pitesti in order to counter-attack the enemy, who had broken through the mountain barrier down the Jiu Valley, with a view to restoring the situation and relieving the Cerna Group. Two events prevented the execution of this plan, the first being the turning of the line of the Olt at Caracal by von Schmettow's Cavalry Corps; the second—and far more serious—being Mackensen's advance across the Danube further East.

As previously stated, the Austrian Danube bridging train had been sent to the vicinity of Sistovo prior to the commencement of hostilities. There it had lain hidden behind some islands in Bulgarian territorial waters for over three months, though its presence had become known to the Rumanians. It may be mentioned that this part of the river was particularly favourable for a crossing; in fact, it had been utilised for this purpose by the Russians in 1877 and again by the Rumanians themselves in 1913. From about the beginning of November, Mackensen's Danube Army, consisting of the 217th German Division, the 26th Turkish Division, the 1st and 12th Bulgarian Divisions, with a composite Cavalry Division (von der Goltz), had been concentrating. All preparations for the crossing had been carefully worked out, river gunboats and monitors had been collected, and it was only a question of waiting until Falkenhayn's Army was near enough to hold out a hand in order to set the whole plan in motion.

Movements of enemy troops towards the Danube had been reported to Rumanian Headquarters by French aviators, and also by a British air patrol from Lemnos; but it does not appear from the Rumanian dispositions that any precise information of that matter had been received by their intelligence service, for the 18th Rumanian Division on this front was split up by brigades from Oltenitza to Turnu Magurele,

---

[1] It was partly on his advice that the Cerna Group had been ordered to maintain its position after the defeat of Targu Jiu—an unfortunate decision.

a front of some 90 miles, whilst the reserve, consisting of the 2nd Cavalry Division, was near Bucharest. It must also be mentioned that this same 18th Division was composed very largely of elderly men most indifferently armed—even according to Rumanian standards—and equipped with obsolete artillery. Moreover, the Austro-Bulgarian river fleet had complete local command on the water. In these circumstances the crossing of the Danube by Mackensen's Army presented no great military difficulties and affords no criterion of the possibilities of the defence of a river line under modern conditions where close watch from the air can be kept on the enemy's movements on the far side of the obstacle.

The crossing was preceded on the 22nd by bombardments at various points from Giurgevo as far as the confluence of the Olt, where a few infantry were put across. On the 23rd, favoured by a thick morning mist, the real crossing commenced in boats, barges and launches. A covering force was soon landed practically unopposed. As visibility increased, powerful artillery fire from the water and from the southern bank broke up any Rumanian attempts at resistance, and by 3 o'clock Zimnicea had been taken by the 217th Division and a special covering force. By next morning a strong bridgehead had been formed to cover the construction of the heavy bridge and this was completed by the evening of the 25th, a praiseworthy engineering performance, as it involved a length of 1,000 yards. The main body then began to cross, the cavalry advancing towards Alexandria, the 217th Division towards Toporu; whilst the two Bulgarian divisions kept closer to the Danube, their right flank protected by the flotilla.

On the evening of the 26th the situation was as shown on Map 10, when von Schmettow's Cavalry had gained touch with the Rumanians at Rosi de Vede. The German advanced guard was approaching Draganesci on the main road to Bucharest; the 217th Division was to the south-east of the cavalry; on their right again came the two Bulgarian divisions; whilst the 26th Turkish Division was following the cavalry, standing some distance back. Meanwhile Giurgevo was being heavily bombarded from the south bank of the river. The Rumanian 18th Division and 2nd Cavalry Division had endeavoured to hold up the advance on the line of the Teleorman, but their flank had been turned by von der Goltz's cavalry higher up the river. They were now holding Draganesci, threatened by von Schmettow, von der Goltz and the 217th Division. It was quite obvious that, without reinforcements, the Rumanian forces opposing Mackensen's Danube Army (Kosch) would be quite unequal to the task.

On the same evening, 26th November, von Schmettow's two cavalry divisions and the 109th Division of Kuhne's Group, Ninth Army, were well across the Olt; the 11th Bavarian Division was following them, but the remaining two divisions, the 41st and 301st, were delayed by broken bridges and were only just beginning to cross the river. The 115th Division was still a day's march west of the river. Half

Kuhne's Group was, therefore, temporarily out of action. Sixty miles further north, von Dellmensingen's group, now 3½ divisions strong, was only just beginning to emerge from the mountains at Curtea d'Arges; whilst Morgen, with two divisions, was still held up in front of Campulung. Morgen, von Dellmensingen and Kuhne were thus out of co-operating distance with each other, though the last-named's cavalry had established connection with the Danube Army (Kosch).

Leaving the Germans, let us now look at the situation from the Rumanian standpoint. When General Presan, the successful Commander of the Fourth Rumanian Army, arrived at G.H.Q. on 21st April, whither he had been summoned to re-establish the Western Rumanian front, he was presented with the aforementioned plan for a counter-offensive across the Olt, and accordingly he proceeded to Pitesti, where the available reserves were being concentrated. On the 23rd, however, news of Mackensen's crossing of the Danube was received, and G.H.Q.'s plan was, accordingly, thrown into the melting pot to be re-cast to meet the new situation.

The position of Mackensen's Danube Army was pregnant with possibilities. It was within two long days' marches of Bucharest, whereas the First Rumanian Army and the left flank of the Second Army wanted at least six days to extricate themselves from the mountains. For the evacuation of wounded, stores and *impedimenta* generally, only the Pitesti–Bucharest line was available; and, as can be seen from the panorama map, the lines of retreat of the Rumanian forces round Rimnik Valcea, Curtea d'Arges and Campulung all led towards Bucharest. If Mackensen were allowed to occupy the latter city, a disaster of the first magnitude would surely overtake the Rumanians. Obviously, he must be stopped, and the best chance of doing so effectively was to attack him.

As will be seen from Map 10, Mackensen's group, if not in the air, was certainly somewhat far advanced, and there existed a bare possibility that it might be crushed before any considerable portion of the Ninth German Army could intervene effectively. Part of this latter army was, in fact, advancing very slowly, and two days' delay had already been gained owing to the destruction of the bridges at Slatina and Dragasani. The German columns further north were still separated by mountain ridges and, consequently, it might be possible to beat the enemy in detail, whilst still spread out on a front of over 150 miles, on the lines so ably demonstrated by Falkenhayn in Transylvania.

A start must obviously be made with Mackensen's group. The defeat of this latter might at best paralyse the whole German strategy, just as the battle of Cibiu had terminated the Rumanian offensive. At the worst, it was the surest method of gaining the time required to withdraw the First and Second Armies to Bucharest. It was true that time was not available to concentrate the necessary striking force before launching the attack, and it would be necessary to concentrate its elements on the actual field of battle. This course would entail a very accurate estimation of time and space as regards both the Rumanian and enemy movements.

General Presan's plan was, roughly, as follows :—
(a) The First Army (14th, 8th, 1st/17th, 13th and 1st Cavalry Divisions) was to delay von Dellmensingen and the 301st Division (4½ divisions), falling back gradually on to the line Tiganesti–Costesti.
(b) On their right the Second Army was to cover the oil regions, Buzau–Ploesti–Targoviste.
(c) In the South, Joncavescu's group, consisting of the 18th Division and some odd brigades, was to stop Mackensen's Danube Army.
(d) The gap of 30 miles between these two groups would tend to diminish as the First and Second Armies fell back, and its security was entrusted to the 1st and 2nd Cavalry Divisions.
(e) Under cover of this screen, a "mass of manœuvre," consisting of the 9th/19th, 21st, 2nd/5th[1] Divisions was to attack Mackensen's left flank from the north, whilst the Russians assailed his right.

The 7th and 10th Divisions would be available later in general reserve; the Russians were asked to send five divisions, and arrangements were actually made with General Belaiev, Russian *liaison* officer at G.H.Q., to move up the 30th and 40th Russian Divisions which were watching the Danube further east. The combined attack was timed to take place on the 30th November.

The success of this scheme, an operation on interior lines comparable to Napoleon's plan in the Waterloo campaign, depended on the following factors :—
(1) The forces detailed to hold off the various groups of Falkenhayn's Army should be adequate for the purpose;
(2) The striking force should be of sufficient offensive power to obtain a decision within the time gained by the holding force.

Unless these conditions were satisfied, there was an obvious danger that von Dellmensingen might advance and threaten the attacking force from the north, or that Kuhne might appear like Blucher on the flank of the Rumanian "mass of manœuvre."

If the forces detailed to hold up von Dellmensingen and Mackensen's Danube Group on the flanks might be considered adequate, the cavalry opposing Kuhne in the centre seems to have been decidedly weak for the purpose, especially as the 7th and 10th Divisions (infantry) were not yet ready to support them. The First Army was, however, told to watch its left flank, so the gap would tend to diminish as the

---

[1] Not included in the first plan.

retirement proceeded; more was apparently expected of the Rumanian Cavalry—or less of the German Cavalry—than was actually realised. Nor was the composition of the " mass of manœuvre " such as to inspire any great confidence. The 2nd/5th Division, formed from units which had fought in the Dobrudja, had been constantly marching and countermarching. It had to be brought across from the First Army, a march of between 40 and 50 miles. The 9th/19th Division, moreover, formed from troops which had been involved in defeats in the Dobrudja, was further weakened by the withdrawal of one brigade to Joncavescu's group. The 21st Division from the Predeal Pass, now near Bucharest, was strong, but became prematurely engaged in extricating Joncavescu's group and stopping Mackensen. The 2nd Cavalry Division south-east of Bucharest was fairly fresh.

The " mass of manœuvre " did not present the appearance of a strong team, but unfortunately it was the best obtainable.

Events from 27th–30th November leading up to the Battle of the Arges or Neajlov. (Map 10.)

To continue the story. Whilst the Rumanians were organising their " mass of manœuvre," Kosch's Danube Army had been steadily advancing. On the afternoon of the 27th, the advanced guard of the 217th Division struck across from Toporul on to the main road at Prunaru, thus cutting the line of retreat of the Rumanians holding Draganesci. Part of the Rumanian 21st Division was sent south to eject the enemy, and the village was taken and retaken, victory finally resting with the Germans when their heavy artillery got up. In this action they took 700 prisoners and 20 guns, and badly mauled the already exhausted 18th Division. The 21st Division had, therefore, to be employed frontally to hold the German advance instead of waiting to strike its flank. Of the other units of the " mass of manœuvre," the 9th/19th Division was coming forward through Coleasca on the 28th, and von der Goltz's cavalry, finding itself between its left and the right of the 21st Division, had to retire hurriedly. On the 29th again the German cavalry was in difficulties from the same cause. Curiously enough, this does not seem to have given the Danube Army any inkling of the Rumanian plan, for on the 30th (Map 11) its advance was continued towards Bucharest, and the crossings of the Neajlov were forced by the three leading divisions, the 26th Turkish Division following on the main Alexandria-Bucharest road, with von der Goltz close in, covering the left flank and out of touch with Kuhne's Cavalry.

In the meantime, Kuhne's group had not been idle. Covered by a number of small cavalry columns consisting of cavalry, one or two guns and some infantry in lorries, it pushed forward practically unopposed, and the advanced guards of the three centre divisions—11th Bavarian, 109th and 41st—had with the 6th and 7th Cavalry Divisions reached the positions shown on Map 11 by the evening of the 30th. Some inconvenience had been caused to the advanced guards by the passage across their front of the 2nd/5th Rumanian Division, marching from near Costesti towards Draganesci; and on the 30th the 6th German Cavalry Division had a fairly serious collision with the same division, being driven back on to the 11th Bavarian Division. The advanced guard of this latter was also roughly handled, losing artillery, machine guns and transport. That the Rumanian movement should have been carried out so far with success is only less remarkable than that it should have occasioned no special concern to Kuhne. Despite the unfortunate experiences of the 11th Bavarian Division, he appears to have thought that it was a question only of wandering detachments of Rumanians which had been effectually disposed of.

Thus on the evening of 30th November, *i.e.*, one day late, the "mass of manœuvre" had reached its appointed area of deployment some ten miles north of, and parallel to, the Draganesci–Balaria road On the right stood the 2nd/5th Division, with its left on Flamanda; next the 9th/19th, with its left on Clejani; then the 21st Division astride the main road north of the Neajlov, and lastly the 2nd Cavalry Division behind the 2nd/5th Division.

We thus get the almost Gilbertian situation shown on Map 11 which discloses a crescendo of enveloping attacks. The German 217th Division was now preparing to push forward to Mihalesci in an endeavour to turn the Rumanian flank on the Arges, while the Rumanian "mass of manœuvre" was about to strike the 217th Division's flank; meanwhile Kuhne's three divisions and two cavalry divisions was advancing, almost unopposed, into the gap between the First Rumanian Army in the north and the rear of the "mass of manœuvre," quite unconscious of any danger threatening Mackensen. As a matter of fact during all this time low clouds, mist and rain made conditions extremely unfavourable for air reconnaissance. Those who maintain that in future nothing can be hid from the air forget that there is such a thing as winter. To complete the picture, one must add that the long-deferred Russian offensive in Northern Transylvania, designed to cut the communications of all the enemy forces operating against Rumania, had at last started on 28th November. It resulted in bitter fighting, some small gains, the withdrawal of one and a half Austrian divisions from Transylvania. Then it gradually petered out, as the Russian divisions were necessarily withdrawn to stem the *débâcle* in Rumania.

On the front of the First Army von Dellmensingen had advanced up to the Rumanian selected position, Tiganesti–Costesti, while a flank column, pushing eastward, had threatened the rear of the Rumanians holding the Campulung Basin and forced them to retire, thus releasing Morgen's group from its long imprisonment in the mountains.

1st December. (Map 12.)

In accordance with the optimistic orders issued on the evening of 30th November, both Mackensen's Danube Army and Kuhne's group continued their advance at an early hour. The "mass of manœuvre" had now cleared the latter's front, and the German columns met with little opposition from the Rumanian cavalry. But things went very differently with the Danube Army. The German 217th Division commenced by making good progress against the 21st Rumanian Division, when at 10 a.m. its Commander, von Gallwitz, received warning from von der Goltz's cavalry that strong Rumanian forces (9th/19th Division) were advancing from the north. A weak flank-guard was thrown out hastily to join hands with von der Goltz's cavalry which was falling back on Ghimpati, and the heavy artillery, which had run out of ammunition, together with all *impedimenta*, were cleared back to Pingalesti.

Further back the 26th Turkish Division began to form front towards the threatened flank to meet the attack of the 2nd/5th Rumanian Division. The latter took Tarnava and claimed to have routed the Turkish Division, which from later events seems to have been a grave overestimate of the actual success gained. In any case the Turks were still holding Draganesci on the main line of communication, when a fateful order reached the Rumanian General Sodec, commanding the 2nd/5th Division. This order, sent also to the 9th/19th Division, was to the effect that he was to direct his advance so as to assist the 21st Division, which had been driven back from its appointed position and was in danger of defeat.

The result of this order is plainly seen on Map 12. The 2nd/5th Division stopped its operations against the Turks and counter-marched. The 2nd Cavalry Division, whose duty it was to protect the exposed flank of the 2nd/5th Division, conformed and, after doing nothing all day, eventually took up its position behind the infantry. Thus the 26th Turkish Division was given complete freedom of action, as was also the German Cavalry.

Meanwhile, the 9th/19th Division, advancing in two columns towards the front Ghimpati–Balaria, was also drawn off to its left owing to the enemy's success against the right of the 21st Division at Mihalesci. However, in an attack at 10 p.m., it captured Balaria, and so cut the main line of communication between the bulk of the 217th Division north of the Neajlov and von der Goltz's cavalry and the 26th Turkish Division south of that river. Communication between the 217th Division and the Bulgarians on their right was also partially interrupted by the 21st Rumanian Division, which had pushed a column forward from the Arges. Further to the south-east the Russian 40th Division was coming into action against the extreme Bulgarian right. Thus. strategically, the requisite combination of all available forces on the battlefield had apparently been effected satisfactorily by the Rumanian Command, but the tactical execution was hardly up to the same standard. All three divisions of the "mass of manœuvre" were converging on the weak 217th Division, which was acting like the cheese in a mouse trap. They were tending to become congested in a comparatively small area, whilst leaving to the enemy comparative freedom of action to form a larger circle round them.

During the night, the 217th Division evacuated its forward positions and concentrated to the rear towards Banesci, a movement which was interpreted by the Rumanians as a presage of victory. But if the local situation may have appeared satisfactory to the Rumanians, the general picture certainly gave no cause for congratulation. The nearest formation of Kuhne's group (11th Bavarian Division) was only one day's march away near Coleasca; two more divisions, the 115th and 109th, were within two days' march, whilst the German cavalry could, if necessary, reach the battlefield. Moreover, 1st December had been a bad day for the First Army in the north, from which the 14th Division emerged only some 1,400 strong, whilst the combined 13th/14th Division could only muster 5,000 combatants. The 1st/17th had, indeed, held up the 301st German Division, which was trying to turn the southern flank, but the whole of the First Army was in retreat towards Gaesti.[1] Part of the scanty general reserve, the 10th Division, had to be called upon to check the enemy's advance and to gain time for the " mass of manœuvre " to complete its task.

The orders issued by the Rumanian Command to the " mass of manœuvre " on the night 1st–2nd December, were to the following effect :—

(i) The 21st and 9th/19th Divisions were to pursue the enemy in a south-easterly direction, so as to drive them into the arms of the Russians who were to form the other arm of the pincers.
(ii) The 7th Division was to cover the operation by holding a position facing north-west between the Arges and Neajlov.
(iii) Similarly, the 2nd/5th Division was to take up a position astride the main road through Ghimpati facing south-west, and the 2nd Cavalry Division was to fill the gap facing west.

Had these orders been carried out, subsequent events would have taken a different course; but, unfortunately, communication with the 2nd/5th Division was interrupted by the small active German cavalry columns, and the order never reached General Sodec, who apparently was left with the dominant idea that he was to march to the help of the 21st Division.

Let us now look at the situation from Falkenhayn's point of view. On the 30th November his Army, the Ninth, had passed from the command of the Archduke Joseph, who had succeeded the Archduke Charles, to that of Mackensen. Early on 1st December, the latter informed Falkenhayn that he intended to seize Bucharest. As neither Bulgarian nor Turkish troops were suitable for the purpose, he directed Falkenhayn to send the 11th Bavarian and 115th Divisions to join the 217th Division, whilst the 109th Division was to approach Bucharest from the west and north-west. Falkenhayn replied that the 11th Bavarian

---

[1] It was in consequence of these moves that the Rumanian staff officers carrying an important order, referred to later, drove into the arms of the advancing enemy.

Division was in action and the 115th not yet arrived. This conveys a strange impression of the German intelligence service, and more particularly so in view of their unchallenged air-superiority. It also shows that, excellent commander as Falkenhayn undoubtedly was, he was a distinctly trying subordinate. However, the situation was completely disclosed at 5 p.m. on the 1st by the purely fortuitous capture of a car containing two Rumanian staff officers bearing an order from the First Rumanian Army Headquarters to one of its divisions opposing von Dellmensingen, and forwarded by the latter to Falkenhayn.

The order ran as follows :—

> "When the 'mass of manœuvre' is ready to-day, 30th November, it will commence its offensive towards Draganesci against the enemy forces which have crossed the Danube. The task of the First Army is to maintain its present positions and hold fast the enemy forces opposed to it. It is most important that its operations should be as aggressive as possible, so as to cause the enemy to employ his whole strength against it.
>
> "Particular attention must be paid to the left flank. The Army Reserve at Gliganu, 10 kilometres east of Cotesti, is at the entire disposal of the Army. ··· On the battle which begins to-day depends the fate of our country. I ask every officer and man to die at his post. I remind all that no mercy will be shown to cowards. All such will be shot without regard to rank. ..."
>
> (Signed)   Lt.-Colonel GOVONESCU, C.G.S.,
> for General Stratilescu,
> Comdg. 1st Army.

A more complete "give away" it would be hard to imagine, and there instantly springs to mind the military axiom that nothing should be contained in an order which it is not necessary for the recipient to know. Was it essential for the Northern Group to communicate to its troops the time and objective of the southern offensive? If so, was it necessary to commit the detail to writing, and could not it have been communicated equally well verbally?

The Germans now had a complete picture of the Rumanian plan from the most authentic source. To this misfortune has been attributed the Rumanian failure. This is undoubtedly going too far, though what actual difference the captured order made is less easy to estimate. Falkenhayn already knew that there were some enemy between his right and Mackensen's left. Writing after the event, he says that the fact did not disturb him, since by continuing to advance eastwards he was most likely to round up the opposition; he assumed, apparently, that the Danube Army would not, in the meantime, suffer defeat. Information received by the evening of 1st December would, however, have disclosed that the latter was being seriously attacked; and, since Falkenhayn was under Mackensen's command, he would eventually have had to obey the latter's demands for assistance from Kuhne's group. Still, Falkenhayn was of an obstinate disposition and did not obey orders gladly, so it is quite possible that he would not have changed his instructions for 2nd December as quickly as he actually did. In that case the Rumanian " mass of manœuvre " might have had another 12-24 hours in which to gain a decision. Whether that would have been sufficient the reader will judge for himself. If not, the Rumanian situation might have been actually worse, as Kuhne's group would have been further east and the direction of its attack more fatal.

This, however, is conjecture. The cold fact was that Falkenhayn, on the evening of 1st December, was basing his plans on a certainty such as seldom falls to the lot of a commander in war. He understood the difficult situation in which the Danube Army temporarily found itself, and the exposed position of the Rumanian forces attacking it On the other hand, the Rumanian Northern Armies were obviously showing signs of giving way completely. It was a case of *embarras de richesses*.

To cut off the retreat of the Rumanian First Army, it was necessary for at least part of Kuhne's group to move to the north-east. To help Mackensen and cut off the southern group from Bucharest, it was equally obvious that Kuhne should advance to the south-east. To do both meant advancing in divergent directions. Falkenhayn's solution of the problem for 2nd December was to direct his northern division to the north-east towards Titu, with an independent mission to attack the left rear of the First Rumanian Army, whilst his two southern divisions (109th and 11th Bavarian) were to march south-east and to attack the Rumanian southern group in the rear. The Cavalry Corps was to cover the 30 miles gap in the centre and try to cut the Ploesti-Bucharest railway; the 115th Division and a Cyclist Brigade, 20 miles back, were to form the Army Reserve.

It would appear that, had the Rumanians at this juncture disposed of sufficient fresh divisions, Rumanian or Russian, and advanced into the gap, they would have been able to turn the tables by attacking in flank either of Kuhne's widely separated columns. Mackensen apparently feared some such danger, since he declined to agree to the 109th Division moving south-east; instead, he ordered Falkenhayn to keep it in the centre, where in the end it did nothing, thus greatly weakening the German counter-attack against the Rumanian southern group, and possibly saving them from a worse disaster than they actually suffered. His fears proved groundless for, in actual fact, the only Rumanian reserve available, the 7th Division, was hurried forward by battalions as it arrived to close gaps in the line between the First Army and the " mass of manœuvre."

The 30th Russian Division was still detraining south of Bucharest, and its commander declined to put it in piecemeal; whilst other Russian formations, at last under orders for an area east of Bucharest, were only beginning to arrive in their usual leisurely fashion.

2nd December. (Map 13.)

During the night the German 217th Division managed to withdraw its forward detachments and concentrate round Banesci, the movement confirming the Rumanian view that they were in full retreat. The Rumanians early on the 3rd continued their attacks, and both the 9th/19th and 21st Divisions gained considerable successes, capturing prisoners and guns. Stilpu was taken at noon, and the 217th Division was practically surrounded. Unaware of G.H.Q.'s intentions, the 2nd/5th also pushed forward, converging on the 9th/19th and leaving its own rear completely unprotected. It may be added that only one Russian Division had shown any activity, and that arm of the pincers had failed to cause the Bulgarians[1] any very real anxiety.

Though the position of the German 217th Division north of the Neajlov was precarious, it had again absorbed the united energies of three Rumanian divisions. The latter had gained a purely local tactical success, quite incommensurate with the risks run to obtain it.

Meantime the 26th Turkish Division, with the main Draganesci–Balaria road at its disposal, had succeeded in deploying and in forming a front which threatened to overlap and outflank the right of the Rumanian "mass of manœuvre." The 11th Bavarian Division was in touch on their left in a still more threatening position. The efforts of the 2nd Rumanian Cavalry Division, which had tried to check them on the line of the Slavaciocul, had not appreciably delayed their advance, and von der Goltz had also again come forward.

The sands were running out.

Unless some more efficient protection than the 2nd Cavalry Division could be provided for the flank and rear of the entangled mass presented by the 21st, 9th/19th and 2nd/5th Rumanian Divisions, it was obvious that a disaster was inevitable. Fortune, too, was against them, for their communications were cut by the German cavalry, and neither orders nor ammunition could be got through to the 2nd/5th Division. In the meantime, in the north the First Rumanian Army had continued its retirement after another trying day, in which the 8th Division and the 13th/14th had again suffered heavily. The 10th Division had, however, successfully delayed the advance of the 41st German Division across the Arges towards Titu, and thus given time to the remainder of the 1st Army to fall back to a position to the west of that place.

The 109th German Division and 7th Cavalry Division had got a footing across the Arges and were in contact with portions of the 7th Rumanian Division. The 6th German Cavalry Division was near enough to co-operate with the 11th Bavarian Division.

---

[1] The Rumanians were under the impression that there was only one Bulgarian Division present, which fact may partly account for their optimism at this stage.

3rd December. (Map 14.)

Unconscious of the actual position of affairs, the "mass of manœuvre" continued its attacks on the morning of the 3rd. Considerable success crowned their efforts. Chirculesti was captured by the 21st Division; Joncavescu's group carried Singureni, while the 9th/19th gained ground towards Banesci. Further east the Russians made progress.

Meantime the storm had been gathering behind the Rumanians, and about 11 a.m. it broke. Unexpectedly attacked in rear, the 2nd/5th Division was seized with panic, broke through the 9th/19th Division and fled across the Arges. The 11th Bavarian Division, with the 6th Cavalry Division on its left, advanced against the 9th/19th from the west, the 26th Turkish Division from the south, whilst von der Goltz and the Landsturm joined in. The unfortunate Rumanian Division, tied up around Stilpu and Epuresti, continued to resist till nightfall, when the survivors made their way across the Arges. The 21st Division managed to retire in fairly good order, as did Joncavescu's group, the Russians on its left conforming.

The Danube Army was too exhausted to take up the pursuit, and according to Falkenhayn was also engaged in the more congenial task of collecting booty which really belonged to the 11th Bavarian Division. The 6th Cavalry Division, which had marched on the morning of the 3rd from a point ten miles to the north-west, was also held up by detachments of the 7th Division some distance short of Mihalesci bridge, which accounts for the escape of a portion of the 9th/19th Division.

Alone the 11th Bavarian Division was unable to force the Arges crossings on the 3rd.

Further north the 7th Rumanian Division delayed the 7th Cavalry Division and 109th Division; whilst, thanks to the stand made on the 2nd by the 10th Rumanian Division, Titu was only taken after the bulk of the First Army had fallen back east of the Titu–Targoviste railway, thus evading envelopment from the south. But all the Rumanian divisions had suffered very heavily, and those opposing Morgen not less so. Thus, when the Germans drove them out of Ploesti on the 6th December, the 22nd Division had only 1,000 combatants and the 12th not many more. The retreat of the 4th Division was intercepted and it surrendered at Mislea on the 7th December. Of the mass of manœuvre, the 2nd/5th Division rallied only 150 infantry; the 9th/19th 4,000 out of 16,000 with which it went into battle. The 18th, 21st and 7th Divisions lost over 50 per cent. Thus the German claims of 20,000 prisoners and 100 guns were probably not exaggerated.

Before completing the melancholy story of 1916, a few supplementary remarks must be made on the Battle of the Arges. The Rumanian operation has been represented as a brilliant example of the use of interior lines, which only just failed to produce decisive results. It has even been compared to the Battle of the Marne, where the interposition of French and British forces between von Kluck and von Bulow led to the retirement of the whole German front. The comparison will not bear examination, however, because at the Marne our flanks on either side of the gap were more than holding their own, which was not the case here. Marshal Foch's axiom that the front must be stabilised before a counter-attack is launched had not been observed.

Undoubtedly, the over-extension of the German forces between the 26th November and 30th November—14 divisions and 3 cavalry divisions on a front of about 180 miles—invited defeat in detail, had the Rumanians been in possession of the necessary means for the purpose and able to bring them to bear effectively within the time at their disposal. The possibility was so obvious and alluring to the Rumanian General Staff, that it tended to obscure the fact that without Russian assistance their means were inadequate for the purpose. Whether they received any definite promises of strong and timely Russian support is doubtful. In any case, limitations of transport made it tolerably certain that it could not arrive until the mass of manœuvre was fully committed on its desperate venture. The whole operation thus became a gamble of the first order; the fact that it started 24 hours late, and that the enemy by the capture of the fatal order looked over their cards, merely converted a probable failure into a certainty, since all the elements necessary for success were lacking.

The amputation of a limb of the German Armies was a delicate surgical operation requiring a far sharper instrument than the Rumanian Army.[1] Fresh, well-trained troops, adequately supplied with a powerful artillery, might have been able to crush in Mackensen's flank on 30th November and 1st December, and then have turned to meet Kuhne's attack on 3rd December. A few tanks to break up quickly the weak flank guard which held up the mass of manœuvre on 30th November might have been decisive. It would be a mistake to argue from this example that such an operation is doomed to failure. In future campaigns it may still be possible by surprise attacks of this nature to obtain a favourable decision quickly. If so, the operation on interior lines as practised by Napoleon may regain the pride of place from which the resisting power of small arm weapons has tended to oust it. In the present instance, the Germans were on perfectly safe ground, for, with the Rumanian Army as it was, there could be no real danger of its obtaining a tactical success quickly, if at all. When criticising Rumanian strategy, this unfortunate fact must be remembered, for no strategy can succeed against consistent tactical failure.

Though it arrived late, the "mass of manœuvre" marched well enough to the battlefield—particularly the 2nd/5th Division—but its subsequent tactical performances were lamentable. The whole Rumanian

---

[1] For instance the 2nd/5th Division, a day or two before it marched south, had been issued with new French machine guns, which the men did not understand and for which ammunition was lacking. They were thrown away early in the battle.

plan was based on the capacity of the 21st Division to hold its ground on 1st December. Its failure to do so led to an unfortunate change in the direction of the attack, to which fact may be largely ascribed the subsequent disaster, aggravated by neglect of elementary military precautions for security on the part of the 2nd/5th Division. The cavalry throughout compared unfavourably with the German cavalry opposing them. The Russian co-operation was slow and half-hearted. But, whilst in such circumstances it is not difficult to show that the Rumanian plan had no great chance of success, it is far more difficult to suggest any alternative which could have proved more effective in saving Bucharest or been equally successful in achieving the partial extrication of the First and Second Armies. Had the 2nd/5th Division received the order to act as a defensive flank on 2nd December, the " mass of manœuvre " might well have been withdrawn without suffering disaster, after achieving a limited tactical success. The alternative plan, favoured by the Russians amongst others, was to remain on the defensive, preferably but not necessarily so as to cover the capital, and there to await the German attack or the Russian counter-offensive in Transylvania, whichever came first. That the latter would ever affect the situation was very doubtful, and, if the Rumanians could not hold disjointed attacks against prepared positions in the mountains, what chance had they against the Germans, when the latter were concentrated and able to develop the full force of their overwhelming artillery? The Rumanians themselves believed that the Germans had none! Their situation may be compared to that of the Germans on the Western Front after 8th August. The Command had lost confidence in the troops, and the troops in themselves. A tactical success was the best—probably the only chance—of regaining both. Acting defensively, the best the Rumanians might have hoped for, in view of the leg-weariness of the Germans, would have been to hold the line of the Jalomita, if indeed the Russians could have been induced to fight so far forward. The slowness of the latter, due largely to faulty communications, had spoilt every plan as soon as it was made and rendered the task of the Rumanian High Command extremely difficult, if not impossible. In practice, the arrangement by which all Russian troops in Rumania came under Rumanian command worked far from well. The situation went from bad to worse as, contrary to the original estimate on which the military convention was based, the numbers of Russian troops had to be continually increased. Such difficulties are inevitable in the case of allies; the Germans also were by no means free from them. But they are apt to assume larger proportions when things are going wrong.

The effective use made by the Germans of their strong cavalry during the preliminary phases in the favourable conditions which obtained will have been noted. The successes of their small mixed columns, which, appearing and disappearing like will-o'-the-wisps, bewildered the heavier and slower-moving Rumanian columns, were marked. The

Germans, however, failed to get full value from their cavalry in exploiting the victory of the Arges.

But perhaps the most remarkable feature of the Rumanian Campaign of 1916 was the influence of the German heavy artillery. At Turtukai, during the battles in the Dobrudja, at Cibiu (Hermannstadt), Brasov, Kronstadt and Targu Jiu, it was the force of the heavy artillery which decided the issue. The desperate Rumanian venture on the Arges was partly caused by their fear of the effect of the heavy guns in the plains. On the Western Front the troops had learnt to dig themselves in before the heavy artillery reached any big development. In the moving battles of the Rumanian Campaign, we get perhaps a better picture of the effect of heavy shell in open warfare, a lesson which is apt to be forgotten in peace time. Moreover, the development of mechanical transport makes it tolerably certain that in any future war on a large scale the employment of heavy artillery is likely to increase.

The remainder of the story can be quickly told. On 3rd December it was decided to evacuate Bucharest and to declare it an open and independent town—a wise conclusion. Its occupation became a race between Falkenhayn and Mackensen, which the former claims to have won by a short head.

For the Rumanian Army there could be no further question of offensive action; the whole front was swinging backwards on the firm pivot provided by the Ninth Russian Army on the Moldavian crest of the Transylvanian Alps. Moreover, the vexed question of the command as between Russians and Rumanians was now settled by Brussilof taking over the whole front to the Black Sea. The Rumanian theatre thus became in name and fact what strategically it should always have been, viz., a portion of the Russian front. Since the Russians did not possess the means, even if they had the desire, to embark on an offensive in Rumania, they fell back on the only sound strategic alternative, viz., to shorten the front as much as possible and to cover with the minimum of troops the reorganisation of the Rumanian Army which, rightly or wrongly, they held to be an unreliable instrument and incapable of further efforts. That this policy met with the most violent opposition from Rumania need hardly be mentioned, since it involved giving up to the enemy all but a small corner of that country. It has been represented as the crowning act of a calculated course of treachery; and, unfortunately, the Russian side of the story is never likely to be represented authoritatively.

In conformity with this policy, preparations were made by the Russians for gradually taking over the whole front. As a first step, they brought up a Cavalry Corps to maintain connection between the Russian IVth Corps, which had been fighting south of Bucharest, and the VIIIth Corps concentrating north-east of that town. Incidentally, the orders for these movements fell into the hands of the Germans.

The latter were directed to pursue with the utmost energy, but performance fell considerably short of the expectations of the Higher

Command. The reasons for this were not far to seek. Kuhne's group, for instance, had been marching and fighting continuously for 26 days and had covered over 200 miles. The men were in rags and their boots worn out. The Cavalry Corps was in no better condition, the shoes dropping off the horses. Under the heavy traffic, the roads became quagmires; supply trains could not get up owing to broken bridges; the bridging trains themselves were far behind. In addition, the Russian and Rumanian rear-guards, fighting by day and retiring by night, inflicted considerable loss on the advancing columns which could with difficulty deploy off the roads. Consequently, the Germans succeeded in cutting off no considerable formation with the exception of the 4th Rumanian Division. In this fashion, sufficient time was gained to rob the enemy of some of the fruits of victory. The oil wells were destroyed or damaged; enormous stores of corn were burnt; arsenals were dismantled or blown up, and factories of military value rendered useless. In addition, the 1917–1920 classes were evacuated, with 30,000 interned enemy subjects, as well as large numbers of civilians, the total being estimated at over $1\frac{1}{2}$ millions. The actual retreat was carried out in the most painful conditions. The two single lines of railways were blocked by the Russian reinforcements constantly arriving. The roads, encumbered by every kind of transport, presented the same pitiful pictures of flying inhabitants as were witnessed in Belgium and France in August and September, 1914, with this addition that it was winter and the weather at its worst.

For some time the German High Command appear to have cherished ideas of effecting a minor Tannenberg by smashing the pivot on which the retreat was being conducted and cutting in across Northern Moldavia. With this object, on 18th December the First Austrian Army with 11 divisions was directed to push forward through the Ghimes and Oituz Passes and get behind the Russians, who had organised a position west of the Sereth (Map 14), whilst Falkenhayn attacked them from the south-west and in the direction Rimnicul Sarat–Focsani. The operation resolved itself into a straightforward attack on a 50-mile front, somewhat on the lines of a battle on the Western Front, and it is not proposed to describe it in detail. The salient features were that, owing to the slow advance of Falkenhayn's Army, the battle (Rimnicul Sarat) only commenced on 22nd December.

By means of the Alpine Corps and two other German divisions, an effort was made to drive in the Russo-Rumanian right in the mountains, in conjunction with the Austrian First Army, but little progress was made. Mackensen, further South on the right, did nothing to help; and it was only after four days' hard fighting that the Russians were ordered to retire to a second prepared position covering Focsani, their right still resting securely on the mountains to the north, but leaving 10,000 prisoners in the enemy's hands.

In reporting the battle to G.H.Q., Falkenhayn thought it necessary to include the following remark: " So long as it was only a question of overcoming Rumanian resistance on the Sereth, we could count on the reasonable probability of reaching and crossing it before the depth of winter. The arrival of strong Russian forces has changed this. It seems possible that the army will be frost-bound before it reaches the river, *i.e.*, before it has broken through the Russian bridgehead, and certainly before it can cross it. The consequences as regards supply, communications, fuel, etc., in this exceptionally poor country, which has been systematically devastated by the Russians, need not be pointed out. The troops in bivouac have already suffered severely." He then asked for clear instructions as to what the objective of the Army really was. He observed that, whilst G.H.Q. apparently wanted him to push north-east in co-operation with the First Austrian Army, Mackensen was continually ordering him to detach troops south-east to help his own operations towards Braila which were going none too well. G.H.Q. replied that the intention was to take Focsani first, and then decide further action. There was no intention, however, of advancing beyond the Sereth—a statement of policy which Falkenhayn describes as " oracular."

Preparations were, however, made to attack the second Russian position or bridgehead, and the battle of Focsani opened on 3rd January. It partook of much the same nature as the previous battle. The operations of the two first days caused heavy losses with no advantage gained. Falkenhayn viewed the situation with considerable misgivings. Discipline in the Army was weakening; stragglers, plundering and looting, filled the towns and villages behind. Typhus and cholera had made their appearance. All his Corps Commanders were of opinion that their men had had more than enough. Only one fresh division remained in reserve, and it looked like a bad ending to the victorious campaign of the Ninth Army. However, G.H.Q. had already announced to the world that Focsani would shortly be captured, and there was no choice but to go on.

On the 5th some success was gained, but this was offset by a Russian counter-attack which made a big bulge in the German centre and captured some heavy artillery. To Falkenhayn the situation looked serious, and he had actually issued orders for the withdrawal from the line of two divisions to attack the flanks of the salient after the Cambrai model, when a Russian order sent out by wireless was intercepted and deciphered. By these means, it was ascertained that the successful Russian attack was not intended to break the line, but rather a local effort to re-establish the bridgehead; it had only advanced so far owing to the unexpected retirement of the Austrian brigade opposed to it. Previous orders were at once cancelled, and divisions were re-grouped on the 6th for a continuation of the main offensive, assisted by a snow-storm which precluded any possibility of a Russian attack.

On the 7th considerable success was gained, the Russians falling back beyond Focsani and retiring across the Sereth and Putna. Further north, however, the Austrians made no progress, and the general strategic situation was not materially altered. G.H.Q. optimistic as ever, now requested Falkenhayn to force the Putna in order to command the railway junction at Maracesti; but the Russian strategy of retirement, until the enemy was too tired to follow, was once again to prove effective. The Ninth German Army had been fighting and marching for three months, and in so doing had, in Falkenhayn's opinion, reached or even passed the limit of human endurance in open warfare. He therefore replied that his troops were exhausted and that the weather precluded further campaigning; he would, therefore, try and reach the line of the Putna and Sereth, which seemed the best defensive position, and there dig in. This was effected without further fighting, and so closed the first year of the campaign.

Remnants of the Rumanian Army had taken their share in the battles of the retreat, but as a fighting force it practically ceased to exist. For instance, after the Arges one weak division could alone be formed from the three divisions of the mass of manœuvre. Of the original 600,000 comprising the Field Army, only about 200,000 remained. Eighty thousand were prisoners in the hands of the enemy; over 150,000 were dead, or wounded and missing; 150,000 more were wandering about or trying to find their units. From the 200,000 survivors, five divisions were formed, which took their places in the line; the remainder went into cantonments, to form the nucleus for the new Rumanian Army which was to rise like a phœnix from the ashes of the old.

The retirement from Wallachia also entailed the evacuation of the Dobrudja, and by the end of the year the last Russian troops had crossed the Danube. Herded together in the small north-eastern corner of Moldavia were now very large numbers of Russian troops, over a million refugees, and the *débris* of the Rumanian Army. Typhus became rampant; then, as the enormous influx from outside ate up the resources, famine followed.

The Rumanian Army lost during the winter 1916–17 more than 100,000 men, a large proportion of whom belonged to the young classes now being incorporated. Mortality amongst the civilians was appalling.

On the other side of the front, conditions were equally cruel for the Rumanians. The badly-fed prisoners in the hands of the enemy died off in thousands; the civilian population was decimated. Even the Ninth German Army, living in the best conditions obtainable, lost in one cold snap effectives equal to more than one-quarter of its previous battle casualties.

Such were the conditions in which the reconstitution of the Rumanian Army was undertaken. Munitions were poured into the country by the Allies, and, with the devoted assistance of a strong French Mission under General Berthelot, a new Army of 15 divisions, admirably equipped and animated by the highest spirit, was ready by the spring. The Central Powers were thus foiled in their object of eliminating Rumania.

Here we must leave the Rumanian Campaign. Space does not

permit of more than a reference to the glorious battles of Marasti and Maracesti, in July and August, 1917.

The Bolshevik Revolution in November, 1917, completed the disintegration of the Russian forces in Rumania. It was followed by a declaration of war by the Soviet Republic on 26th January, 1918, which led to Rumania having to fight against enemies on every side. At the end of March, 1918, she was forced to make a preliminary peace with the Central Powers,[1] which was finally ratified in May. But Rumania was again to take up arms early in November in a last and successful effort to secure her territorial war aims.

In comparison with the population, the Rumanian losses from 1916–19 were very large, dead alone being 2,330 officers, 217,516 other ranks, including 169 officers and 70,335 other ranks who died as prisoners in enemy hands. If to the above be added the victims of plague, pestilence and famine, the total loss of Rumanian life has been put at 800,000,[2] or more than 10 per cent. of the population.

Before closing this summary, let us try to strike a balance of profit and loss caused by the intervention of Rumania on the side of the Allies. The Central Powers had gained moral and political advantages, and a much-needed fillip had been given to their national *morale* after the defeats of Verdun, the Somme, the Trentino, the Izonzo, and in Galicia. In a military sense, communication with Turkey down the Danube had been opened; while materially the Central Powers had acquired grain and oil, though not so much as they had expected. On the other hand, it is quite possible that Germany would, in any event, have carried out an offensive in the Balkan theatre, and in view of the difficulties of maintaining any large forces on the Salonika front, it is probable that this offensive would have taken the form of an attack on Rumania. Falkenhayn states quite frankly that the advantages of invading Rumania had been considered as far back as the spring of 1915, and again in the autumn of that year.[3] Obviously, if carried out at Germany's selected time, greater results would have been obtained with far less effort.

As it was, the campaign strained the German resources very considerably; the losses, which fell mainly upon German troops, were far from negligible even in 1916,[4] and heavier losses were still to come before Rumania was eliminated from the war. The invasion inflicted hardships on Rumania, probably surpassing those suffered by any other of the combatants, with the exception of Serbia, but they were not all loss from the general standpoint of the Allies, and in the long run proved to be the birth pangs of the " Greater Rumania " of to-day.

(*Finis.*)

---

[1] An armistice with Germany was made on 16th December, 1917.
[2] " Istoria Razboiului." Vol. II., page 644.
[3] " General Headquarters, 1914–16, and its critical decisions," pp. 203, 204.
[4] The Germans themselves are unable to say what they actually were.

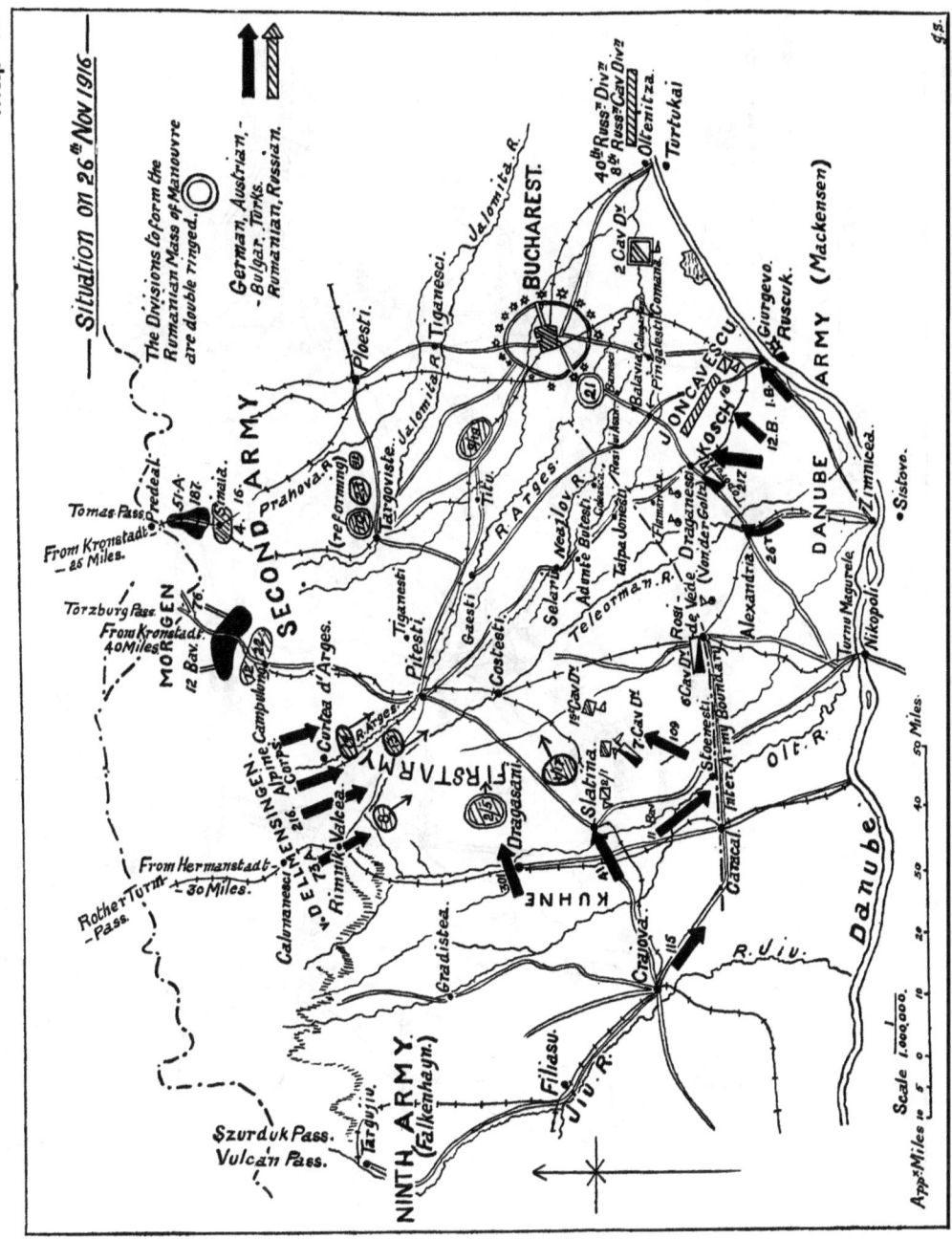

Map 10

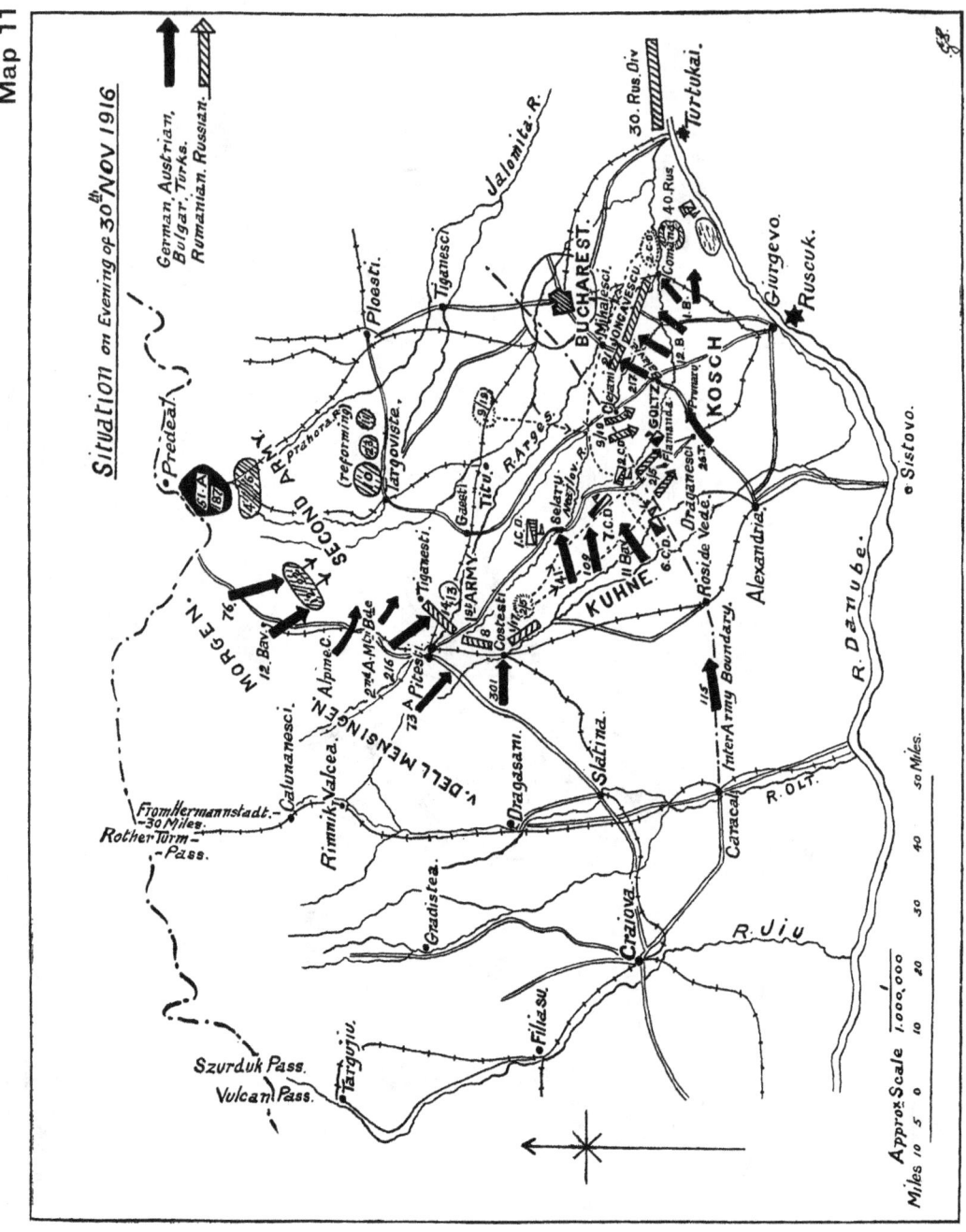

Map 11 — Situation on Evening of 30th Nov 1916

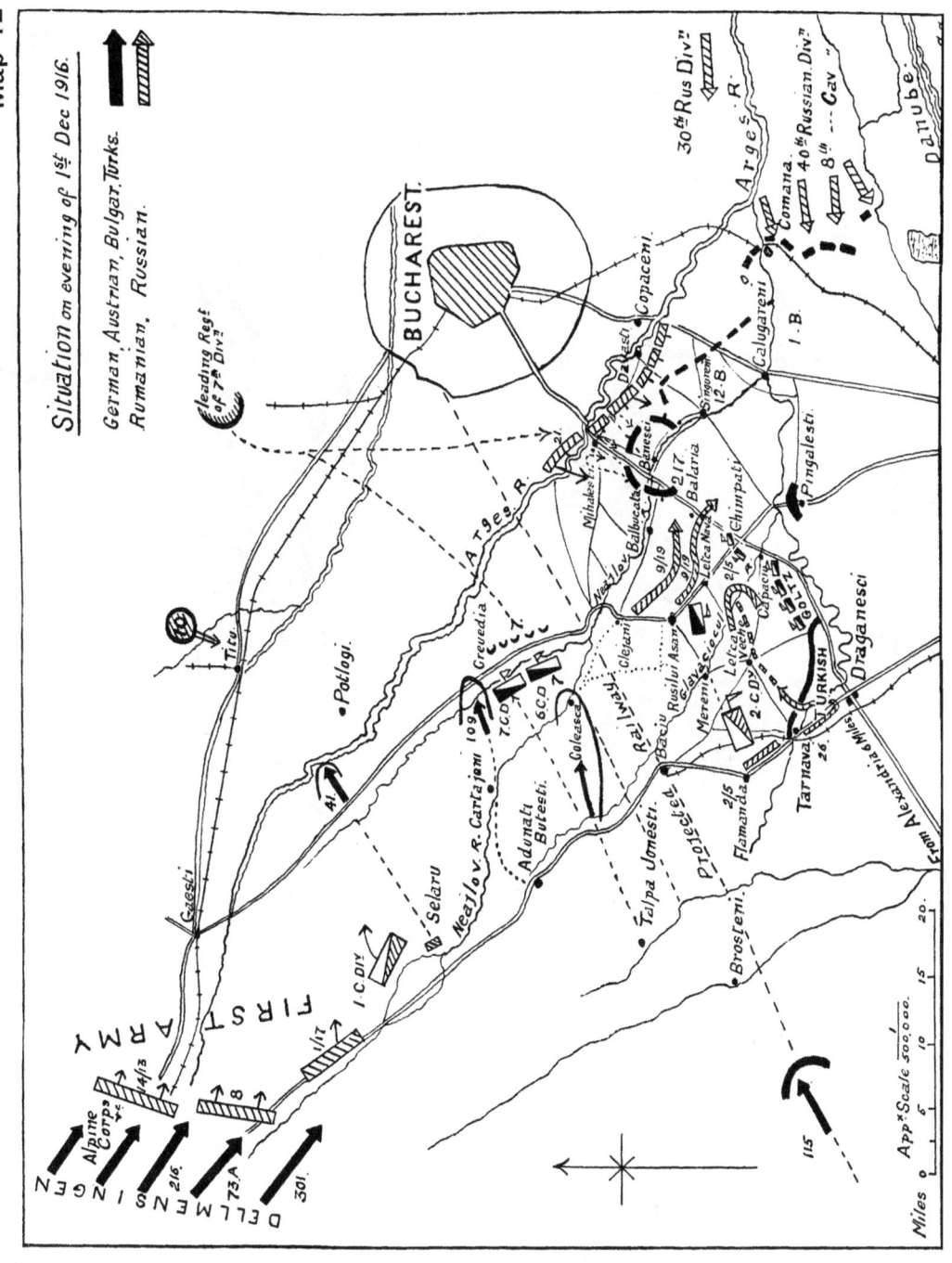

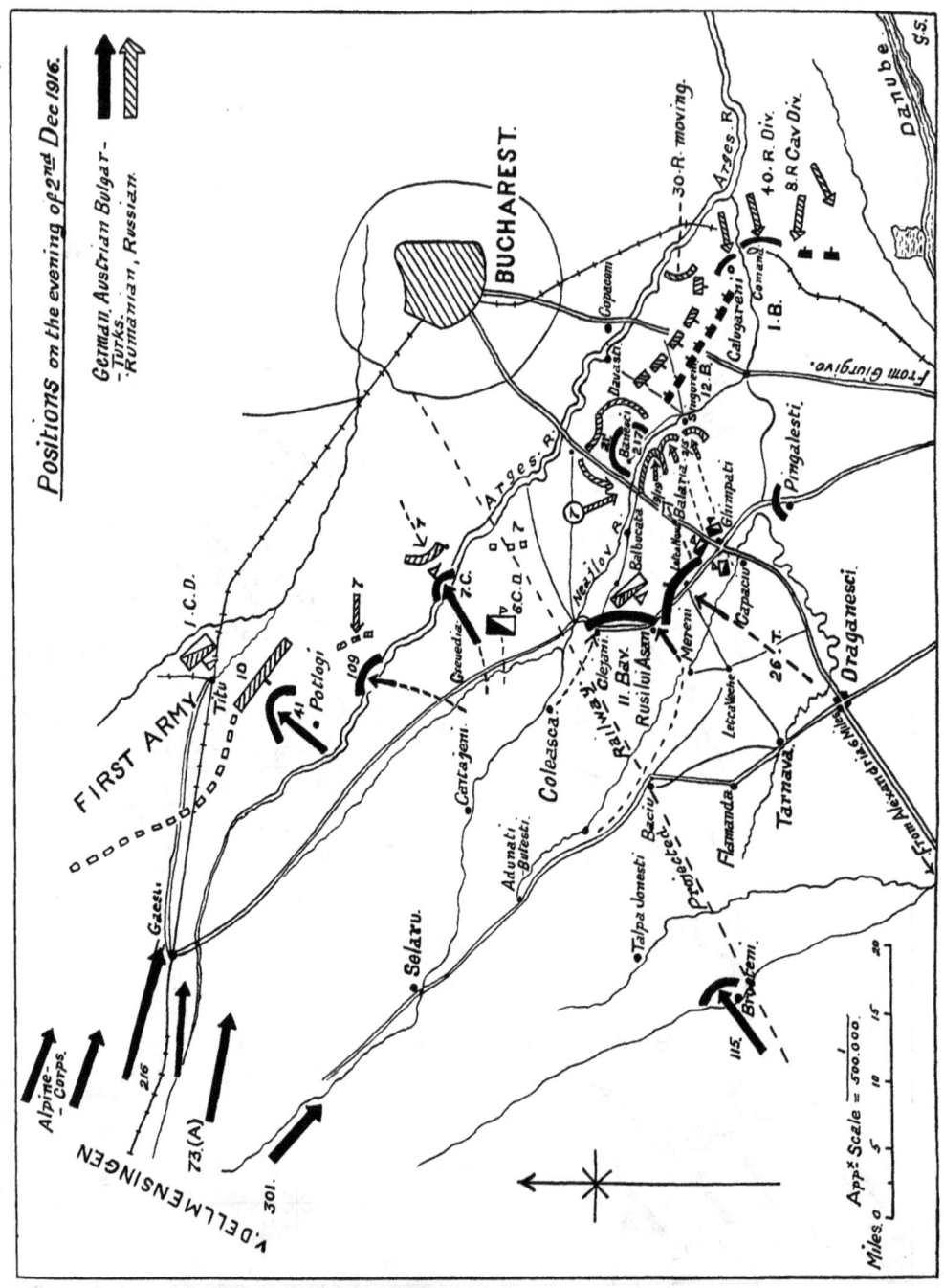

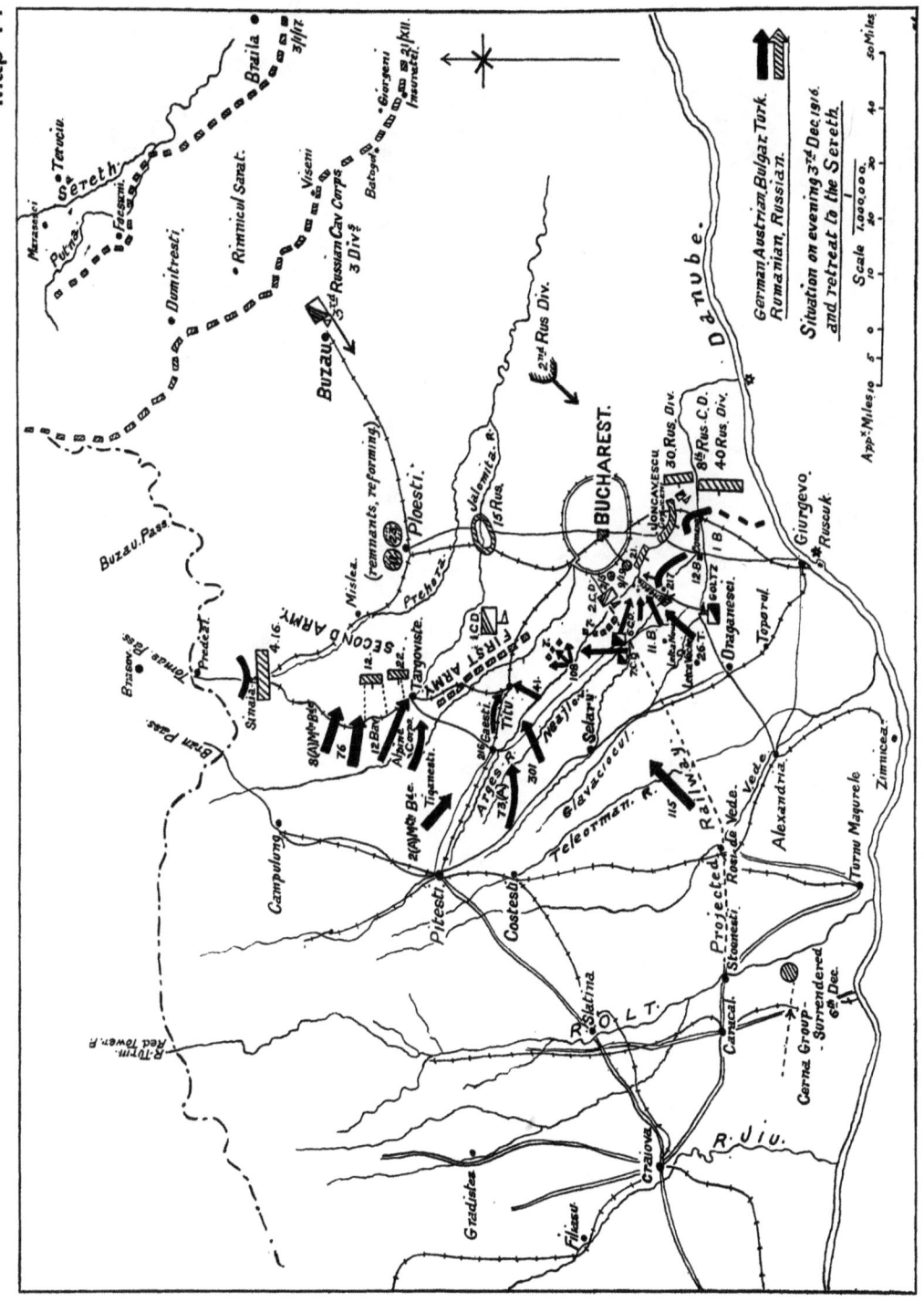

www.ingramcontent.com/pod-product-compliance
Lightning Source LLC
Chambersburg PA
CBHW080407170426
43193CB00016B/2839